Outbelieving Existence

Editorial Board

Literary Criticism in Perspective

* * *

About *Literary Criticism in Perspective*

Books in the series *Literary Criticism in Perspective* trace literary scholarship and criticism on major and neglected writers alike, or on a single major work, a group of writers, a literary school or movement. In so doing the authors — authorities on the topic in question who are also well-versed in the principles and history of literary criticism — address a readership consisting of scholars, students of literature at the graduate and undergraduate level, and the general reader. One of the primary purposes of the series is to illuminate the nature of literary criticism itself, to gauge the influence of social and historic currents on aesthetic judgments once thought objective and normative. Another purpose is to show how literary criticism has enhanced our appreciation of literary works by revealing their underlying structures and themes.

What works for me . . .
is this: is with me:
Is a body outbelieving existence
The shining of perfection, the myth-chill.

James Dickey, "The Lyric Beasts"

This book is dedicated to Janet, who curves with the world to outflesh and outspirit him who sits loosed and hawking.

Gordon Van Ness

Outbelieving Existence: The Measured Motion of James Dickey

CAMDEN HOUSE

Copyright © 1992 by
CAMDEN HOUSE, INC.

Published by Camden House, Inc.
Drawer 2025
Columbia, SC 29202 USA

Printed on acid-free paper.
Binding materials are chosen for strength and
durability.

Printed by Thomson-Shore, Inc.
Dexter, Michigan

ISBN:1-879751-27-5

Library of Congress Cataloging-in-Publication Data

Van Ness, Gordon. 1950-
    Outbelieving existence : the measured motion of James Dickey /
Gordon Van Ness.
            p.   cm. -- (Studies in English and American literature,
linguistics, and culture)
    Includes bibliographical references (p.   ) and index.
    ISBN 1-879751-27-5
    1. Dickey, James--Criticism and interpretation. I. Title.
II. Series.
PS3554.I32Z93   1992
811'.54--dc20   92-17370
                                                             CIP

Contents

Foreword

THIS BOOK OVERVIEWS THE scholarship and criticism on the writings of James Dickey. That he remains a striking presence on the contemporary American literary scene and that he continues to experiment with language and technique mitigate the efficacy of such a study. Criticism—and the effort to survey and synthesize it—is always an on-going endeavor. Nevertheless, in the more than thirty years since Dickey's first volume of poetry appeared, particular critical approaches or hypotheses have established themselves, and certain assumptions have become commonplace, which this book examines and compares.

Clichés of acknowledgment rhetoric are sometimes accurate. I am thankful to my colleagues at Longwood College, who have enabled me to do my research. Geoff Orth, Chair of the Department of English, graciously provided all that I dared ask for. Michael Lund and Ellery Sedgwick read and critiqued chapters and in so doing improved the manuscript. I have relied on their sound judgment. Vera Williams, Dean of the Graduate School, awarded me a faculty research grant, which facilitated my completing this study on schedule. Bill Frank, Dean of the School of Liberal Arts and Sciences, and Massie Stinson, my faculty mentor, offerred counsel and encouragement. They believed.

Chris Langner of Computer Services not only provided me with an IBM PC but also unselfishly gave of her time to format the manuscript and answer my frantic questions regarding WordPerfect. Her patience and computer knowledge command my admiration.

Norma Taylor and Florence Southall consistently secured the books and articles necessary to assess Dickey scholarship. Their prompt and relentless pursuit of my requests was invaluable. Angelin Brewer and Jennifer Steib also located important articles or reviews when they could least afford the time.

Joyce Pair inspired me to measure the motion, and Marvin and Syrl Cohen kept me from breathing too rarified an air.

Benjamin Franklin V said No when he had to and Yes when he did not. He has my deepest gratitude and respect.

My interest in James Dickey began in 1982 when I read *The Zodiac* and realized that words matter. They open possibility. Then I read *Poems 1957–1967* and my work was determined. My parents, believing literature is not practical, have extravagantly supported what they consider their oldest son's strange obsession.

Gordon Van Ness
March 1992

Introduction

THREE DECADES OF DICKEY scholarship have revealed a body of writing remarkable for its diversity. While early critics quickly identified Dickey as a distinctive new voice, noting his prominent themes and their biographical underpinnings and romantic links, later studies have failed to scrutinize his mature efforts as thoroughly. Some works have received examination only or primarily in reviews. Perhaps not surprisingly with a writer who continues to experiment with poetic and fictional techniques, this commentary has largely contented itself either with discussions of previously determined concerns or, less critically, with general summaries. While Dickey's induction into the American Academy of Arts and Letters reflects a recognition of his literary achievements, it is also true that critics believe his more innovative work much less successful than the early poetry, often because they judge it according to standards and techniques Dickey initially established for himself. In attempting to reach the sublime, some assert, he has often approached the ridiculous, a risk he claims is necessary. In addition, Dickey's large presence, owing both to his barnstorming tours in the sixties for poetry and himself and to his Rabelaisean experiences, has contributed to the tendency to confuse the man and his work. Critics have occasionally focused as much on his life style as on what he has written, a proclivity which has mitigated the serious scholarly attention the work deserves.

This study endeavors to complement Dickey's existing canon by examining its critical reception and reputation and by placing that response in a chronological and methodological context. The book's organization into nine chapters that survey the poetry, fiction, and non-fiction prose, as well as Dickey's own criticism, provides a systematic means to comprehend the scholarship. Because Dickey's poetry so often shows aspects of the mythic rites of passage, involving a departure, an initiation, and a return, its discussion here follows a similar division or pattern. Dickey has always viewed himself primarily as a poet, though he has willingly explored the possibilities of other genres. To understand the artist, the full scope of his creative efforts requires examination, though criticism of Dickey's children's poetry and non-fiction prose, in particular, remains scant and largely superficial. One of the conclusions determined by this study of the scholarship is that critics have offerred no single, encompassing literary theory or hypothesis by which to understand all Dickey's work. Perhaps that is to be expected for a writer who claims to be a bundle of contradictions and whose life, he has stated, is "more complicated and unknowable than that of Lawrence of Arabia" (*Sorties* 89). Nevertheless, seminal studies by H.L. Weatherby and Joyce Carol Oates become indispensable, and many specialized investigations which focus on individual poems, such as Ross Bennett's essay on "The Firebombing," go a long way toward comprehending what

Dickey himself calls "the motion" of his work. They render the task of students and readers new to Dickey's poetry an easier endeavor.

In providing an orientation and direction to the scholarship, this critical overview also attempts to reveal those areas where original study or further scrutiny remains. Only when Dickey's work receives complete examination will his achievements receive the recognition they merit. This book begins to measure the motion.

1: Departure: *Into the Stone, Drowning With Others,* and *Helmets*

SCHOLARS HAVE FOCUSED LITTLE critical attention on *Into the Stone* (1960), perhaps because, after omitting one-third of its poems from *Poems 1957-1967* (1967), Dickey overlooked the volume completely when putting together *The Early Motion* (1981), the collection which depicts the youthful phase of his writing career. While *Drowning With Others* (1962) and *Helmets* (1964) suggest stronger poetic control of form and meter as well as imagery and theme than *Into the Stone,* the first volume clearly presents Dickey's emerging voice, his emphasis on direct experience and the complex of emotional and physical responses that act as ritual to invite a transcendent communion, particularly with the dead. The volume also identifies, even proclaims, his thematic concerns: family, war, death and dying, and love. Dickey attributes the book's division into titled sections to John Hall Wheelock, then the editor of Scribner's *Poets of Today* series, declaring in 1970: "I had no notion that that would be of advantage" (*Self-Interviews* 84). The format remained, however, and Dickey kept the divisional scheme for his next two works. Though he eliminated the section titles for these subsequent volumes, the subjects themselves broadened in scope. For example, while the third part of *Into the Stone* presents the demise of family members and friends, death in this section of *Drowning With Others* focuses on the surrender of consciousness to a dream-like state or magical moment in which rational faculties are suspended. The poems in the third section of *Helmets* then assume varied and unique perspectives, such as an unspecified being, a bum, a snake, and a sleeping child. Death imagery, including graves, candles, prayers, and coffins, links these poems into a coherent grouping. Unfortunately, no critical study presently exists that thoroughly develops these acknowledged themes through Dickey's early motion.

Dickey's initial creative efforts resulted from a new, heightened perspective of the world. At North Fulton High School in Atlanta, his interests centered primarily on football, track, motorcycles, billiards, and girls. Because he felt poetry attracted women, he became intrigued by it. Poetry, Dickey relates, "was just something to make me interest*ing*, and in the process, I got interest*ed*" (*Self-Interviews* 24). Yet if his adolescent years were undistinguished, his decision at the age of nineteen to leave Clemson A & M in December 1943 after only a semester of college and to enlist in the Army Air Force initiated experiences that he regarded in retrospect as vital rites of passage. Departing from a safe, Southern provinciality, he entered a world war as part of the 418th Night Fighter Squadron and experienced in his aerial missions of the Pacific campaign feelings of immense power. In *Self-Interviews* he asserts:

> There's a God-like feeling about fighting on our planet. It's useless to deny it; there is.... You can never do anything in your life that will give you such a feeling of consequence and of performing a danger-ous and essential part in a great cause as fighting in a world war. (137-38)

Dickey concludes, "You feel a nostalgia for war because all the intensities of life, youth, danger and the heroic dimension, as nearly as you will ever know them in your own personal existence, were in those days" (138). The remorseless brutality of combat, however, also caused a strong sense of personal guilt, both because of the deaths Dickey anonymously inflicted during his air missions and those of close friends such as Donald Armstrong, whose plane crashed during a strafing run. He was captured and beheaded by the Japanese. When Dickey entered Vanderbilt University in the summer of 1946 to complete his formal education, he immersed himself in the writings of anthropologists like W.H.R. Rivers, Alfred Radcliffe-Brown, and Bronislaw Malinowski, and mythologists like Jane Ellen Harrison and Sir James George Frazer. These readings caused him to view his war experience as *rites de passage*, the three-stage quest of the mythic hero that involves a separation, a penetration to a source of power, and a return. Rather than a kind of gambit, poetry now became a giving back or yielding up of part of what he had learned; a poem was valuable in itself. Much of Dickey's early work reflects aspects of this sense of journey. As he states in *Self-Interviews*, "It's not that my experience lent itself more to mythology than anybody else's, but that my own life lent itself to being mythologized just as *much* as anybody else's did" (85).

The full impact of the Second World War on Dickey's early poetry, however, has emerged only recently. Baughman (1985) and Van Ness (1987) both explore the consequences of this combat: the emotional, physical, and psychological dislocation; the pervasive sense of guilt; and the subsequent need to discover sustaining beliefs and heightened forms of existence through ritual and myth. If recent scholarship centers on the biographical and historical origins of Dickey's poetry, initial studies nevertheless note his concern with altered states of being and his need to outbelieve existence. Sustained critical analysis really starts, not surprisingly, only after Dickey won the National Book Award for *Buckdancer's Choice* (1965) and after *Poems 1957-1967* collected poems from his earlier volumes and included a lengthy section of new work entitled "Falling." Critics then began to scrutinize more systematically what his early poetry involves. Only later did they examine particular volumes to highlight the transition of themes or style or to reveal a development in Dickey's search for self or in his psychological recovery from the effects of combat.

Weatherby's (1966) essay, an important early study, correctly perceives Dickey's effort to re-create the world through a mysterious process of exchange involving a man and his opposites. Experiences in Dickey's poems involve not only an individual and an animal, as in "A Dog Sleeping on My Feet," but also men opposed by nationality, men and trees, men and machinery, and even the living and the dead. Initiated by a figurative death, such as sleep, an hallucination, or an incident where reason ceases, the exchange produces a composite vision. In the penetration between the human and the non-human worlds, a new and heretofore impossible perspective results, though this mutual surrender of sensibilities occasionally fails, as in "The Driver" and "The Shark's Parlor." Yet the situations in some of Dickey's early poems often seem staged, affected, and occasionally preposterous, such as in "Springer Mountain." Wendell Berry (1964) argues that the poetic insight that should constitute the essence of the poem here appears deliberately and mechanically contrived. He concludes that nothing mitigates "the inherent silliness and clumsiness.... I have no faith in it, no belief that anybody ever did any such thing" (131). Dickey himself remains undeterred by such criticism, asserting in *Self-Interviews* that "there's a razor's edge between sublimity and absurdity. And that's the edge I try to walk" (65). He adds: "I don't think you can get to sublimity without courting the ridiculous. Therefore, a good many of my poems deal with farfetched situations" (65-66). The poems constitute, in part, a matter of intellectual and emotional curiosity, of seeing what happens when he deliberately places his persona under certain conditions or restraints. This tendency to experiment with subject matter and manner has found its detractors and proponents throughout Dickey's career.

Stepanchev (1965), another early critic, observes that Dickey's subject matter derives from three principal areas of experience. He ignores Dickey's announced scheme and labels these interests as country life, World War II, and family relations. While not tracing these thematic threads, he provides perceptive commentary on the poetic technique, calling it "a compromise between traditional forms and the free forms of the 1960's" (192) and noting the variation of stanzaic length, the use of rhyme to underscore meaning, and the accented measure of three, four, or five beats in the line, what Dickey calls "a night-rhythm, something felt in pulse not word" (*The Early Motion* vii). Likewise, Glancy (1971) surveys the early volumes, but having now the advantage of Dickey's own critical ideas in *Babel to Byzantium* (1968) and *Self-Interviews* (1970), the commentary more fully analyzes the stylistic technique and intent. Attempting to determine "if the poet preaches what he practices" (1), Glancy applies those criteria Dickey uses to judge himself and others.

Discussing the standards for his early motion, Dickey declares his strong dislike of "the element of artificiality" (*Babel to Byzantium* 282) and his desire instead to make "effective *statements*" (285). This effort led to his striving for "a very stripped kind of simplicity in verse" (284), a form characterized by short, usually three-beat lines and refrain lines that serve as a separate, summary stanza of the poem's actions and attitudes. Initially, this use of refrain arose simply from Dickey's interest in poetic experimentation, but the hypnotic beat and incantatory effect also allow the stanza to serve as "a summation or coda" (*Self-Interviews* 85). Moreover, the reader's fundamental interest in "what happens next" caused him to adopt a narrative technique that presents "a fusion of inner and outer states, of dream, fantasy, and illusion where everything partakes of the protagonist's mental processes and creates a single impression" (*Babel to Byzantium* 287). Such a method opens up possibility so that the reader enters into the situation. In *The Suspect in Poetry* (1964), Dickey declares: "What matters is that there be some real response to poems, some passionate and private feeling about them: that for certain people there be certain poems that speak directly to them as they believe God would" (10).

For Dickey, Glancy asserts, poetry represents "a corporeal experience" (2) that intensifies life by awakening the potentiality inherent in common, remembered events. The poet captures the reader through the incantatory sound of short, anapestic lines. Each line is a declarative sentence, and the refrain constitutes a deliberate device to reflect the dream experiences described in many of his poems. Glancy's discussion of *Drowning With Others* also extends Weatherby's (1966) analysis. Like the latter, it discerns the poet's identification with and participation in the natural world, an Emersonian desire to enter nature and achieve, as Dickey writes in "The Salt Marsh," a "marvelous, spiritual walking." The communion results from his empathy with the physical world, his depiction of violence and emotional extremes in "fantastic situations" (16), and his penetration of the past through dream images deliberately juxtaposed with remembered incidents. These memories become more real than the quotidian. Unlike Weatherby, however, Glancy notes that while the metamorphosis often involves Dickey's persona, occasionally it does not, as in "A Screened Porch in the Country." Here he presents heightened perceptions of his family as they simply sit and are observed on a screened porch, their shadows soon lengthening to "enter the place / Of small, blindly singing things." The poet's imaginative insight, not the poet himself, sees the world extended. In *Helmets*, moreover, the poet either literally assumes the sensibilities of another or else completely surrenders his own, as in "Approaching Prayer" and "Springer Mountain." This radical subjectivity effects an intensified and expanded understanding of the physical world, not merely a momentary exchange where the speaker simultaneously becomes both human and non-human, as usually occurs in *Drowning With Others*.

While Mills (1968), like Glancy, attributes Dickey's ability to achieve sustaining connections to the poet's imaginative response to the physical realm, he defines that response more specifically than the latter. Dickey's reaction involves not only the unconscious or irrational part of the mind but also its rational aspect. The heightened state of consciousness, enhanced by the unconscious, produces images that suggest dream, and the deeper this dreamlike atmosphere, the more logical the connections appear to reinforce the sense of reverie. Dickey often uses sleep and night dominated by moonlight, as in "Sleeping Out at Easter." Here his imaginative abilities free the speaker's body from its earthbound limitations and permit "a kind of infinite capacity for extension" (232). "A Screened Porch in the Country," while occurring within the poet's vision rather than involving him directly, additionally locates the human beings in "an entirely different dimension" (232) as a consequence of the imaginative transformation. In the process Dickey reveals a new and larger religious or metaphysical understanding, what Weatherby (1966) terms "the way of exchange" (669) and Bly (1964) the "spiritual struggle" (41) in the poems. Because of his ability to split his intuitive powers between the predator and his prey, particularly in those works involving animals and hunting, and to reveal the perceptions and feelings of each, Dickey represents a poet whose imagination is of "a primitive, magical type" (234).

Mills (1969) also suggests that the poet's imaginative breakthrough into higher consciousness characterizes contemporary poetry in general and is achieved "at great personal cost" (5). Dickey refers to this liberation as "The Second Birth" and claims its origins reside "in the development of personality, with its unique weight of experience and memory, as a writing instrument, and in the ability to give literary influence a new dimension which has the quality of this personality as informing principle" (*The Suspect in Poetry* 56). Achievement of his own authentic speaking voice, the poet's self, involves the power of the imagination to invite or assume the essential being of others as if it were his own, regardless of whether that other is living or dead, human or non-human. Mills asserts: "Ordinary objects, situations, patterns of nature in his poems suddenly assume the conformations of myth or join in rituals of initiation and transformation, interchanging identities, and progressing toward transcendent revelations" (*Creation's Very Self* 19). In "The Dream Flood," for example, from *Drowning With Others*, Dickey imaginatively re-creates archetypal details in a magical cosmos to provide "the aspect of personal myth" (*Creation's Very Self* 19). Emphasizing the extreme subjectivity of contemporary poets, including Dickey, Mills (1975) declares that the quest for personal vision often leads toward a distant and dangerous realm where "the self stands alone, unaided but for its own resources" (*Cry of the Human* 135), an assessment that reinforces Oates's (1974) analysis that Dickey's poetry reveals an evolving search for the poet's own personality.

Noting the highly personal experiences that engender Dickey's poems as well as his conscious manipulation of metrical form, Lensing (1973) argues that while poetic narrative necessarily counterpoints reality and illusion or objectivity and subjectivity, the two realms are never completely segregated. External phenomena cannot be separated from the emotional and imaginative responses they cause. For Dickey the truest reality consists of "empirical reality psychically remade through the imagination" (159), though this creation lacks permanence. Lensing presents an essentially psychological analysis of the early work, as when he states: "Dickey's poems release that which is perhaps most often consciously repressed in human awareness: the association and identification of all that is without with varying levels of emotional distortion" (159). The narrative framework of each poem reveals a complex movement whereby the persona initially provides an orientation to the external setting, then enters into a subjective consciousness of that setting, re-creates it according to "the poet's personal egocentric vision" (160), and finally re-establishes the external setting at the poem's conclusion.

Though warning, like Weatherby (1966) and Wendell Berry (1964), that such a technique may lead to excesses which are offensive or even unintentionally comic, Lensing acknowledges Dickey's own awareness of the risk. While "The Sheep Child" and "Drinking from a Helmet" represent such exaggerated situations, the decision to write poetry that will "involve the reader in it, in all its imperfections and impurities" (*Babel to Byzantium* 290) broadens poetic boundaries to include metaphors that may continually dissolve and then re-emerge in new forms. In doing so, they provide a vital elasticity, a technique that is poetically energizing. Dickey's association with animals derives from this tendency, particularly because the poet recognizes in them "the analogies of human personality, frequently of a higher form" (164). Citing such early poems as "A Dog Sleeping on My Feet," "Springer Mountain," and "The Owl King," Lensing asserts that the poet discovers his own identity through a mystical communion with animals, an exchange that he attributes, like Glancy (1971), to the "associative power of the poet's imagination" (164). The narrative technique also demonstrates Dickey's extreme romanticism; the limits between man and environment dissolve to confront what Dickey calls "the inexhaustible fecundity of individual memory" (*Babel to Byzantium* 280).

The use of narrative to convey the possibility of a vitalized life provides Bowers (1985) with his thesis that Dickey deliberately orchestrates his activities to promote himself, his poetry, and his view of divinity. Noting the "rhetorical packaging" and the "verbal manipulation" (56) of "The Heaven of Animals," for example, he argues that Dickey "sells the poem" (30) along with his mystical vision of a coherent universe. Narrative reflects the most effective means of "pitching" his personal experiences. While Ramsey (1973) argues that Dickey is a lyric poet whose later long poems do not succeed as well as his early short ones, Bowers disagrees. After briefly using the lyric, the poet abandoned it for narrative, a fact apparent when one recognizes that of all the poems in *Into the Stone*, only "The Performance" achieves forceful presentation. Regarding technique, Dickey himself stated in 1971 that he "wants, more than anything else, for the poem to be an experience—that is, a *physical* experience—for the reader. It must be a completed action, and the plunging in of the reader into this action is the most difficult and the most desirable feat that the poet can perform" (*Sorties* 59). This early preference for narrative becomes most explicit when he asserts, "In most of my poems I want a sense of *story*" (*Sorties* 49). While the lyric poet presents a reflection, narrative tells this story and thereby more effectively involves the reader. Bowers declares that after struggling to balance the two techniques, an attempt best suggested by "Sleeping Out at Easter," Dickey abandoned his effort to accommodate the lyric impulse and used narrative poems to heighten his popularity in the 1960s, when he was "moving and speaking among his kind" (*Babel to Byzantium* 256) as he toured college campuses to read his poetry.

In his "Notes on James Dickey's Style," Lieberman (1968) analyzes Dickey's youthful style, but unlike Glancy (1971), attempts more particularly to show a pattern of development, claiming that the early volumes generally reveal "a conscious stripping away of those techniques of style and mental strategies which have grown suspect after repeated use" (57-58). Figures of speech become wed to the narrative events themselves such that they constitute not so much metaphors as extensions of meaning already inherent in the experience, as in "The Performance" when Dickey writes, "blood turned his face inside out" or "sun poured up from the sea." Sense impressions heighten the realism and intensify the poetic experience without the reader's becoming literarily self-conscious. These images provide a deeper, more intense feeling of literalism than mere factual details. The technique serves to "assimilate" (59) the mental anguish and pain that can properly be apprehended only through hallucination. While he makes no effort to impose or even imply a psychological justification for Dickey's style, he does declare: "Excruciating mental experience is translated into exact physical correlatives" (59). Despite Dickey's own commentary concerning his management of line and form, Lieberman characterizes the chief unit of measure as the long sentence, usually extended over several stanzas, and he cites as examples "The Island" and "The Scratch," both poems, however, that Dickey excluded from *Poems 1957-1967*. "Drinking from a Helmet," while containing the sentence rhythms of earlier poems, nevertheless departs from the line and stanza units by having them function as a film strip in which each unit centers on a particular action separate in time from the others. However, the stanzaic breaks or pauses are themselves functional in the overall rhythmic structure so that the poem's movement greatly departs from the "unbroken flow and rhythmic sweep" (60) of most of the early motion.

Spears (1970), who taught Dickey at Vanderbilt, labels him a Dionysian poet whose principal models include Roethke, Lawrence, Rilke, and, quite possibly, Sir Herbert Read. Given these influences, his poetic use of humans and animals reflects not a need to identify the self but an implicit spiritual meaning, much like the classical myths of the centaur and Leda and the swan. The central impulse, therefore, to unite with humans or other creatures at "moments of ultimate confrontation, of violence and truth" (257) is not confessional. While it often exhibits an "openly personal and autobiographic-al" (258) aspect, it nevertheless possesses an essential impersonality by primarily displaying strong elements of ritual and myth that involve forces and powers beyond those of the persona. Often obscure as a consequence, Dickey balances in his best poems these Dionysian concerns of metamorpho-sis and transfiguration with his Apollonian preoccupation with openness and accessibility, attempting to achieve what Spears calls a "Poetry of the Impossible, the burning bush" (260). His concern is with vision, but Dickey recognizes the inescapable problem of form. Because it best conveys a union of opposites, narrative technique becomes more explicit in later poems as he confronts such opposites as the human and the non-human ("The Sheep Child"), the past and the present ("The Leap"), and the living and the dead ("The Bee"). Weatherby (1966) sees Dickey's use of this method as an effort to find the motion held within a still point (671). Ramsey (1973), however, asserts that Dickey is essentially a lyric poet whose principles of form and structure have determined his career: "A great lyric rhythm found him; he varied it, loosened it, then left it, to try an inferior form" (177). Ramsey's detailed analysis of such early poems as "Sleeping Out at Easter" and "Dover: Believing in Kings" explains the power of the lyric rhythm, what he terms "end-stopped rising trimeter" (177) dominated by iambics and anapests that are clearly felt and whose effect is both variable and cumulative. The study, which more thoroughly explicates Dickey's metrical technique than either Nemerov (1963) or Glancy (1971), argues that when Dickey moves beyond the meters in *Into the Stone* or *Drowning With Others* to poems like "Chenille" and "Cherrylog Road" in *Helmets*, into what Ramsey conveniently calls his "middle phase" (180), his basic rhythm loses its essential power. Rising trimeter best serves the incantatory, and because "Cherrylog Road" combines the incantatory with the conversational, the rhythms fail to reinforce the poem's essential strengths. Dickey's "basic form hovers near enough to be felt, sometimes to interfere, but lacks its earlier throbs and dire or delicate changes" (180). Yet Ramsey concedes that the middle phase occasionally works well, as in "The Scarred Girl," where idea and rhythm coalesce.

The stanzaic form of the early motion generally remains open and becomes capable of achieving any movement within tone or theme. The basic structure of "Sleeping Out at Easter," for example, is neither a fully Aristotelian form or argumentative structure nor one moving with an organic inner necessity. Rather, the forms here and elsewhere are freer and less restrictive, but they are always characterized by associative, thematic development where the persona journeys in and out of mystery, dream, or death. Two additional methods also evidence themselves in the early poems. One involves a "semi-narrative of an experience" (Ramsey 188) in which the speaker criss-crosses among objects or beings within the experience itself, as in "Trees and Cattle" from *Into the Stone*. Here, some detail is natural ("A cow beneath it lies down"); some, metaphorical ("I have been given my heart"); some, speculative ("And fire may sweep these fields"); and some, supernatural ("my bull's horns die / From my head"). Poems of this kind usually depict one specific place and are sustained either by a unity of tone, by religious or romantic attitudes, or by the patterned but unpredictable movement among the objects in the work. The second additional method is a direct narrative of an experience which, though literal, conveys meanings beyond itself, as in "The Driver" from *Helmets*. These three techniques best function in short poems. In Dickey's long poems like "The Owl King" and "Drinking from a Helmet," such methods "are virtually all he has to build with, and are not enough" (189).

Ramsey's discussion of the characteristic movement inherent in Dickey's poems, though only part of his analysis of stanzaic form, highlights an important feature of the poet's work. That Dickey titles his initial efforts *The Early Motion*, that he labels his middle period *The Central Motion*, and that his complete oeuvre will become *The Whole Motion* indicate the poet's own sense of the importance of movement. Critical studies consistently emphasize this concern. Rosenthal (1967), for example, declaring that Dickey's work constitutes "an attempt to be guided by afflatus" (325), refers to him as "expansive and energetic" (325). His poetry empathetically connects with "personalities" (325) because, for Dickey, language is "a form of energetic action" (325). While cautioning that this energy sometimes precludes the material from achieving an established shape and meaning so that the poems "tend to grow more than to be shaped" (326), Rosenthal believes, like Lensing (1973), that such dilation characteristically belongs to Dickey's means of discovery and release. Only through such a method can his poetry become "alive with figurative notes of compassion, fantasy, empathy" (325). Kirschten (1988), in his sympathetic exploration of Dickey's "lyric universe" (10), discerns a thematically centered idea of motion in the poet's mysticism, Neoplatonism, romanticism, and primitivism. Two traits, for example, devolve from Dickey's mysticism—the ideas of optimism and monism. These qualities accurately characterize the primary action of a poem like "In the Tree House at Night," where the speaker experiences "a shudder of joy" and then stirs "within another's life." Using "extensive metaphors of motion" (13), as when Dickey observes that the fields become "disencumbered of earth" and the pine cones "danced without wind," he imparts such "expansive unifying movement" (13) that all paradoxes dissolve: "The blanket around us becomes / As solid as stone and it sways." The resulting unity is ecstatic.

This unstated principle of an enlarging unification implies two additional traits associated with mystical consciousness: the absence of a particular ontology or theology and the feeling that one has achieved a special knowledge or revelation. Both also involve or infer motion. Dickey never explicitly identifies the nature of the world's primary energy or power. In "Approaching Prayer," for example, the narrator states, "I don't quite know what has happened / Or that anything has." Kirschten, however, believes it to be a "poetic Absolute of Motion that lies behind appearance and mixes nature and human consciousness" (21). Consequently, the self participates actively and at times passively with what is real and even with what is imagined because such unions bring a poetic response that discerns new meaning. In "The Lifeguard," for example, the persona, while only temporarily bridging the real and the illusional, nevertheless recognizes that nature selects indifferently. And in "Drinking from a Helmet," the young soldier arrives at a knowledge of war and peace, a revelation so striking that he "could have stepped up into air." Yet however joyous, Dickey's mysticism occasionally conveys a sense of violence and danger that contrasts with earlier poems. "The Heaven of Animals" portrays the perfection Dickey envisions as part of the cycle animals experience, but it also displays a heightened anxiety and strain. The predators may leap with "a sovereign floating of joy" and the prey may be "torn" and then "rise, they walk again," but violence is part of the motion. It becomes "an active animating force" (23) within the mystical experience. Carroll (1968) similarly perceives in the poem not so much a mystic communion as "a malevolent tension" (46-47) where the endlessly repeated cycle of predators killing prey who then rise to be torn again suggests "a nightmare—radiant, dignified but a nightmare nonetheless" (47). The poem, far from presenting the union of divine and animal, becomes only "a richly intricate metaphor for human life" (48).

Hodge (1990) believes "The Heaven of Animals" reveals Dickey's conviction that "earth is the only place where his heaven exists" (15). The attitude or philosophy continues a distinctive tradition in American literature in which the natural world becomes the only paradise. Dickey's literary precursors, including Whitman, Emerson, and Thoreau and extending even to Stevens, similarly discern the infinite in the immediate. Yet if heaven is where animals live, then violence also resides there. The poem, Dickey's "most dramatic presentation of his radical vision" (15), implies the immortality of the species, though not the individual. While predators may kill and prey die, "the predation and death are joyous, and so are resurrection and life" (15). For Dickey, therefore, such a condition mandates that the individual actively struggle to participate in the processes of life. Such intense living requires both a full knowledge of this world and a recognition of the inexorable presence of death.

Like Hodge, Davison (1967) considers Dickey's work a search for "heaven on earth"(119). His quest is for order within chaos, attained by seeing the unity between the living and the dead and by finding the relation between the human and the animal worlds. The success of this struggle resides in the discovery of concrete images to express "his mystical intentions" (119), images which probe the layers of reality to reveal a central unity. Drowning and hunting reflect this effort in the early poems because they enable the persona to unite himself with the dead and, in doing so, to enrich nature. Death therefore constitutes not only the "ultimate way of becoming more than the self," a mystical knowledge of the animal world and the animal nature that remains part of humanity, but also "the ultimate kinship" (120).

McGinnis (1975) acknowledges the mysticism inherent in the poems but, unlike Kirschten (1988), focuses not on the primacy of motion but the more basic idea that a reality exists that one intuits rather than intellectually comprehends. Dickey's mysticism usually expresses itself as "an ecstacy" (5) whose origin resides in his need for rebirth and which imparts a feeling of immortality. This mysticism also aligns itself with "a strong paganism" (5) because identification with nature yields a corresponding unity. Echoing Spears (1970), McGinnis calls Dickey's poetry Dionysian but argues that it is not Apollonian because the poet "seeks redemption of the individual, perhaps by destroying him" (6). The Dionysian ecstasy occurs when the persona feels "a mystical union with the One" (8) conveyed by a "bombardment of the senses" (8) that threatens to overwhelm him even as it permits him an entrance into nature. Believing Dickey's mysticism founded on "a monistic ontology in which invisible, secular, implicit motion pervades all things" (24), Kirschten accounts for the poet's efforts to confront and redeem death by arguing that he tries to transform stillness and pain into motion and joy. Dickey's work reveals a transistion from a motion and assimilative principle essentially pantheistic to one where the unifying process becomes an instrument of realistic, personal exchange rather than a cosmic release (24). It is a movement apparent by juxtaposing "Inside the River," a poem depicting a generalized mysticism, to "The Lifeguard," where mysticism renders more particularly the sense of delirium and loss.

Duncan (1964) and Niflis (1972) center on Dickey's concern with death and dying and his identification with the dead. Poems like "The Being" and "Drinking from a Helmet" suggest "an initiation" (Duncan 131), as if the poet himself had crossed into a hidden realm that provides him "a secret commission" (131). In "The Being," for example, the persona recognizes an "infinite, unworldly frankness, / Showing him what an entire / Possession nakedness is," and in "Drinking from a Helmet," his prayer travels "through all the strings of the graveyard" until he realizes "I was the man." Because such poems expose what is real and call forth the individual, they suggest the mysteries of Orpheus, whose music charmed the dead. Niflis argues that often his "preoccupation" (311) concerns dead soldiers and that such a poem as "Hunting Civil War Relics at Nimblewill Creek" infers "a kind of personal apology for a public guilt" (311).

David Berry (1974) greatly expands on this critical approach by asserting that although Dickey joins the world of the dead with that of the living, he not so much achieves a unity as he simply becomes "renewed, nourished" (233). The poems from his first three volumes reflect the nature of the Orphic journey, which consists of "descent, contact with the inaccessible, celebration" (240). In *Into the Stone* such poems as "Orpheus Before Hades," "The Sprinter's Mother," "Poem," "The String," and "The Underground Stream" depict dead members of Dickey's family, and the persona attempts in all but the last of these to achieve communication that, though momentary, becomes forever available through the ritual of ceremony. "The Underground Stream," however, tries to exorcise the memory of Dickey's dead brother, who possesses "a smile of incredible longing" and who desires to "claim his own grave face / That mine might live in its place." *Drowning With Others* suggests that Dickey failed to break this feeling of continuity because "In the Tree House at Night" shows the dead brother's spirit so strongly present that the persona's own self-identity seems threatened. Another poem, "Armor," finally succeeds in exorcising the dead brother's spirit, though he is left questioning who he will be when he dies. In no other subsequent poem, Berry argues, does Dickey deal with "the consummation of oneness" (239) attained between himself and his dead brother. Rather, his concern then centers more on the war dead. Poems such as "Hunting Civil War Relics at Nimblewill Creek," "The Island," "A View from Fujiyama After the War," "Horses and Prisoners," and "Drinking from a Helmet," all from *Helmets*, fulfill the role of Orpheus as the speaker attains an empathetic consciousness that occasionally becomes "harmony with the dead, renewal, and joy" (241). Berry distinguishes "The Driver" and a later poem, "The Firebombing," as works where the Orphic journey fails, for Dickey's persona remains unable to descend into the realm of the dead. Only for his family dead and for those fellow soldiers killed in the war does the poet successfully descend; the realm of the enemy deceased, however, remains closed. More importantly, while the encounter with family dead nourishes the speaker, such nurture lacks the intensity of the celebration depicted in the war poems where the journey salutes death and effects a personal renewal.

Like Kirschten, Varn (1988) identifies motion as the primary thematic concern in Dickey's early poetry but, unlike him, argues that its presence in the poems owes to Dickey's sense of guilt and mainly results from "the responsibility man must bear for his own existence, ultimately for his own birth" (4). Desiring to escape an undifferentiated formlessness, the individual wills himself into the physical realm; but to overcome a subsequent death, he must achieve a unity that precludes such change, a union with the primal natural forces obscured by material concerns and desires. Without this connection, man remains isolated and in conflict with otherness, seeking sovereignty or omnipotence. Birth, then, constitutes "man's basic crime" (4), and he becomes compelled either to seek superiority over the physical or spiritual or to join with them both to achieve a harmonious whole. Calhoun and Hill (1983) agree, asserting that "there is otherwise too much threat of extinction, too much certainty of oblivion" (62). For Dickey, survivorship is possible only when the individual arrives at "a physical and spiritual synthesis that all too often is ignored in the pursuits of material—or weak, ephemeral spiritual—goals" (62). Dickey's poetic motion becomes his attempt to return to a condition that precedes birth and whose perspective accepts both life and death.

Kirschten (1988) declares that motion accounts for other aspects of Dickey's poetry besides his mysticism, including his Neoplatonism, romanticism, and primitivism. Although Covel (1985) has also detected Platonic elements in the early poems, specifically "The Scarred Girl" from *Helmets*, only Kirschten has systematically endeavored to detail this concern. He argues that Dickey's method of combining thematic and emotional opposites resembles the Greek concept of harmony and that his identification with and harmonizing of man and the universe happens within "a causal ontology that at times seems Pythagorean" (26). Though offerring no astronomical theory, Dickey's mystical world suggests a cosmic harmony because it proportions motion and music. In "The Vegetable King," for example, one spring night the speaker sleeps outside in a pine grove and returns the following morning strengthened by his communion "with gods / Which move through Heaven only as spheres / Are moved: by music, music." Through the Platonic ontology of the music of the spheres, Dickey's own poetic motion becomes not simply a cosmic law but also "a mediating magical link between man and nature" (30). At the poem's conclusion, the speaker's emotional state has become directly aligned with the natural order of the universe through Dickey's musical motion. Cosmic harmony is transferred. Similarly, in "Hunting Civil War Relics at Nimblewill Creek," Dickey uses the music of a bird's song to uncover the past and bind the persona and his brother to their Southern forebears: "the cry / ... pronouncing / 'Nimblewill': / Three times, your being changes." This Neoplatonic use of music and motion fully adheres to Dickey's emphasis on rhythms to induce mystical, trance-like states, an effort to bring forward what he calls in the preface to *The Early Motion* "the self-generating on-go that seems to have existed before any poem and to continue after any actual poem ends" (vii-viii).

Covel's analysis details the philosophical and metaphysical aspects far less thoroughly, stating that the primary tenet in "The Scarred Girl" is the Platonic distinction between the physical world and the ideal. Covel agrees with Lieberman (1967) that Dickey's principal problem is accommodating both the inner and outer worlds and discovering the poetic means to unite their antithetical natures. Functioning in the dualistic world of Platonism becomes difficult for Dickey's characters when they confront the finite realm and fail to make it conform to the ideal, to what Dickey calls "the Good, the True, and the Beautiful" (*Self-Interviews* 131). The young woman in Dickey's poem, her face disfigured by an automobile crash, realizes that despite plastic surgery she has "a newborn countenance" and she must now struggle to find an inner beauty. Hers is a new good, one "plainly / In sight, and the only way." Such a redemption in understanding arrives "only through suffering" (26). Arnett (1975) similarly discerns in Dickey's poetry "a search for the Ideal—a search for the ideal woman, a search for the ideal self" (298), and Smith (1981) observes that Dickey endeavors to see "beyond the surface of things" to discover "redemption" (354).

Redemption and renewal remain the prerogative of the romantic poet. In presenting Dickey as an American romantic, Gregor (1977) claims the personae become intimately involved in the transformations that occur when the supernatural expresses itself in nature. Kirschten (1988) asserts that Dickey's mystical impulse becomes romantic as his "targets of exchange" (43) become more specific, a concreteness particularly apparent in his treatment of animals. Dickey's belief in instinct leads him to single out their economy of movement, declaring: "The instinctual notion of how much energy to expend, the ability to do a thing thoughtlessly and do it right, is a quality I esteem enormously. I want to get a feeling of this instinctualness into poetry" (*Self-Interviews* 60). Because it constitutes his ontological imperative, motion affects the metamorphoses Dickey so often depicts with animals. In "Listening to Foxhounds," for example, the persona speculates not on the hounds but on the fox seeking escape by "Leaping stones, doubling back over water." Excluded from the camaraderie of the other hunters, he identifies with the hidden animal in a secret communion. While Dickey here empathetically experiences animal instincts, in other poems the outward surfaces of nature give rise to the radical transformation of the persona. In "Sleeping Out at Easter" the speaker's hand touches "The source of all song at the root," and in "Near Darien" "the wind springs into the sea" and "The moon creeps into its image" to produce an "infinite breath." Such poems present "the surface of Dickey's natural topography" (56) but, as with animals, this almost always leads to heightened experiences. Still other poems like "The Dusk of Horses" portray a persona whose voice seems already to have half-entered the animal realm, into "unthinking nature" (*Babel to Byzantium* 150), to apprehend what Nemerov (1963) calls "the continuousness of forms, the flowing of one energy through everything" (61). Dickey's method of exchange in this poem also involves the qualities of objects, but he now varies the technique by rendering "the essence of a material thing merely one moment in a shared continuum of motion" (Kirschten 62). The discussion of Dickey's romanticism in this regard broadens the perspective of Glancy (1971) and gives Weatherby's (1966) process of exchange its fullest critical extension.

Kirschten's final hypothesis examines Dickey's primitivism of "motion, magic, and ritual" (85). Dickey himself provides the foundation for such an approach when he declares in *Spinning the Crystal Ball* (1967):

> I think that the poetry of the future is going to go back the other way, back toward basic things and basic-sounding statements about them, in an effort, perhaps a desperate one, to get back wholeness of being, to respond wholeheartedly and fullbodiedly to experience, aware all the time that certain constraints must be affirmed.... And if we are lucky in the search, and believe in it enough, we shall at last arrive at a condition of emotional primitivism, of undivided response, a condition where we can connect with whatever draws us. (14-15)

Using Sir James George Frazer's distinction between homeopathic and contagious magic, Kirschten argues that these two magical principles constitute "specifications of his Absolute of Motion" (88), and he cites "Springer Mountain" and "A Screened Porch in the Country," respectively, as examples. Ritual, and the violence often associated with it, are aspects of this magic and evidenced in "The Vegetable King" and "A Folksinger of the Thirties." Noting that Dickey's universe is so much one of passage and exchange that the personae seem to experience transformations of a personal and cosmic nature, Kirschten concludes his hypothesis by stating that Dickey's poetry contains aspects that "powerfully integrate the three major phases Arnold Van Gennep identifies as *rites de passage*, namely, separation, transistion, and integration" (133). For example, "The Hospital Window" depicts the persona leaving a hospital where his father lies deathly ill,

"Drinking from a Helmet" exhibits a transistion as a young soldier assumes the identity of a fellow G.I. recently killed by putting on his helmet, "Springer Mountain" shows a hunter returning to the human realm after enterting the animal world, and "Dover: Believing in Kings" incorporates all three stages. Underlying the *rites de passage* is motion, Dickey's governing principle.

Friedman (1966) similarly observes the violence that attends much of the early poetry, yet concludes that Dickey presents only the appearance of confronting the physical world. Because they deny the danger of directly touching nature, the poems are finally only about themselves: "They lack incisiveness, they lack passion, and they lack genuine climaxes" (56). For example, *Drowning With Others* dwells mostly on animals, birds, and hunting in its first section, particularly with lower life forms, such that the concern amounts seemingly to "an obsession" (56). Although presenting a process of exchange, Dickey often diminishes or distances the terror and violence attending the situations he describes, as in "The Heaven of Animals" specifically. The volume's second section primarily concerns violence, travel, and war, but while complimenting the imaginative conception behind "In the Lupanar at Pompeii," Friedman indicts its language and conclusion, calling the former "fuzzy" and the latter "dissipated in the wateriness of the style" (58). The third section focuses on family, self, and situations around which to spin "dream visions" (58). The book's concluding portion deals with weathers, landscapes, and geographies, but the poems are all "ornamental build-up" (58) that evades climactic insight and recognition. The analysis of *Helmets*, while less condemning, still faults what other critics like Glancy (1971) praise, charging that the poems distort what the persona sees until the vision becomes unclear rather that metamorphosed into significance. When this occurs, Dickey's stanzaic forms become "more flexible and experimental" (60). The volume's four-part divisional scheme concerns, respectively, animals and nature; people and nature; states of dreaming, sleeping, and waking; and "what seems to be World War II" (62). With each of his first three volumes, the poet becomes more explicit in his war poems only by coping with combat "gradually and retrospectively" (62). Friedman's approach is not psychoanalytic; rather, his concern is with style, which he concludes is "lush and woolly" (66).

As Dickey's poetic output increased, critics like Friedman began to assess his position in contemporary American poetry and to distinguish thematic and stylistic development throughout the separate volumes. Bly (1964) claims Dickey's poetry embodies Southern life and culture more than any present or previous writer and, despite the presence of certain faults, Dickey's "great originality" (55) remains noticeable. Davison (1967) contrasts Dickey with Lowell technically and imaginatively and states that his poems initially imitated Muir. Howard (1966) compares Dickey to Jarrell, using the former's own criticism of the latter: "He gives you a foothold in a realm where literature itself in inessential, where your own world is more yours than you could ever have thought, or even felt, but is one you have ever known" (*The*

Suspect in Poetry 84). Kennedy (1964) believes that Dickey, like Roethke, is "a poet in search of an absolute" (5) whose specialty is "psychological adventure" (5). Other critics, however, view Dickey less favorably. In his survey of the poets writing under the Wesleyan University Press label, Friedman (1966) begins directly: "I take up Dickey first because I do not think he is as good a poet as Simpson" (55); and he then baldly adds, "In fact, I don't think he's as good a poet as he's reputed to be" (55). Morris (1969) harshly observes Dickey's "total inability to achieve conciseness within a single poem" (319) and then faults his observations about animals as scientifically inaccurate. Bly (1967) recants his inital praise, accusing Dickey of social and political insensitivity and arguing the deterioration of his poetry to only "a gloating about power over others" (70).

Individual volumes also come under closer critical scrutiny in this reassessment. Despite claiming to address Dickey's poetry generally and *Into the Stone* specifically, Bly (1964) focuses only on the section titled "Death." The poems reveal a preoccupation with the deaths of an uncle and an older brother, experiences which mitigated Dickey's "life-certainty—his assurance that he is really alive" (42), and suggest the belief that the dead have paradoxically become more alive than the poet himself. Van Ness (1989), however, perceives in this volume Dickey's idealization of woman. For example, "Into the Stone" suggests the mythic idea that women are actualizing agents, ideal figures who offer larger possibilities and without whom men remain unfulfilled. Dickey himself notes that the title poem depicts "the quality of a love relationship" as the speaker approaches "the love object, the woman," and he adds: "Not only the world of the person in love is changed by the new love relationship, but the whole universe is changed" (*Self-Interviews* 98). Calhoun and Hill (1983) additionally assert that the poem elevates love to "almost a naturalistic sacrament" (21), while Baughman (1985) states that love becomes "a principal means of countering death" (26) as the poet psychologically re-structures a self fundamentally disordered by combat.

Howard (1966) echoes Bly's (1964) view that the poems reflect a spiritual struggle. They exhibit "the heroic quest which is this poet's unending adventure" (414), one which confronts "love and death, self and circumstance" (414). In particular, *Into the Stone* shows that the Self would escape the ephemeral world and enter an idealized universe, a view similar to that of Varn (1988), but such an entry requires "the mediation of ritual" (415). The titles of many poems in the first volume therefore suggest archetypal events in the Grail legend, including "The Underground Stream" (The Freeing of the Waters), "The Vegetable King" (The Fisher King), "Into the Stone" (The Hidden Castle), and "Walking on Water" (The Bleeding Lance). The poems present a mythical world where everything seems to remain essentially the same and yet constantly change or transform to create "a net of correspondences" (416). Moreover, the personae *become* by paradoxically remaining fixed. Anticipating Kirschten's (1988) emphasis on motion, Howard asserts that "there is no end to action" (416), the gerundive form being utilized to show both rituals of family and kingship and devotions to "the divine Other" (416). While the self always remains in chronological time ("The Vegetable King"), its acts are not historical but rather of ritual and myth ("The Signs") and determined by incantation. Only "The Performance" presents "the rare accommodation of circumstance" (418), a singular event examined through narration rather than ritual. For the most part, Dickey's first volume yields an impression of "liturgical consummation" (418). Occurrences become synonymous with fate such that Howard wonders what initiatory experiences the poet himself has undergone, though he does not explore the inquiry.

Oates's (1974) analysis of Dickey's early poetry assumes this more psychological perspective, declaring that a "ceaseless, often monomanical questioning of identity" (97) characterizes the poems. Like Ramsey (1973) and Bowers (1985), she sees *Into the Stone* as "lyric and meditative" (99), presenting a nearly anonymous persona obsessed by forms who resolves unacceptable conditions or situations through a "formal, ritualistic—essentially magical—imagination" (99). The poet's deep sensibilities cause him to attempt to discover if any metamorphosis or change exists that is more than merely a matter of perspective, more than a question of arranging language. If not, the individual remains fundamentally estranged from himself and the world. Therefore, Dickey continually examines image after image, exploring and absorbing it, only to discard it after its failure to sustain. In so doing, he becomes increasingly self-conscious. While *Into the Stone* most celebrates life, in particular the many forms of love, the volume nevertheless suggests passivity with "no hint of the guilty, pleasurable agitation of physical life" (104). Even in the title poem, for example, the persona is "on the way to a woman," absorbed in his contemplation of the "stone" that is the moon. The poem never presents acts of consequence and finally evidences only a Platonic interest in being.

Also assuming a psychological approach, Baughman (1985) cites Dickey's own statement in *Babel to Byzantium* regarding the autobiographical content of his poetry:

What I have always striven for is to find some way to incarnate my best moments—those which in memory are most persistent and obsessive. I find that most of these moments have an element of danger, an element of repose, and an element of joy. (292)

Declaring his combat in the Second World War as "the most dramatic occurrence" (6) in Dickey's life, Baughman states that the consequent guilt resulted in three stages of psychological progression that define Dickey's poetry: a movement "from static to animating guilt—confrontation, reordering, and renewal" (8). As Dickey examines his major concerns—"war, family, love, social man, and nature" (8)—he explores his evolving understanding of what survivorship means. *Into the Stone* specifically suggests the nature of "the death imprint" (8) caused by his fighting in World War II.

Here Dickey questions not the reality of death but its ontological meaning. In "The Jewel," for example, the speaker feels attracted to the weapons of war, but he cannot determine if he has, in fact, physically survived: "Truly, do I live? Or shall I die, at last, / Of waiting?" His suspension between the living and the dead, moreover, also characterizes family relationships, as in "The String." Although the speaker successfully defeats death in "Into the Stone," he cannot extend that small victory into nature because in "Sleeping Out at Easter" and "The Vegetable King" he remains disoriented, unsure whether life or death holds him. Baughman believes the volume details the initial stage of a process that depicts a "symbolic form of death and rebirth" (7) and that involves confrontation and questioning as Dickey seeks to find renewal.

Calhoun and Hill (1983) emphasize Dickey's use of ritual in *Into the Stone*, declaring that it provides the means by which his four announced subjects mingle with his aggressive desire to access "nature's nonhuman (or primordial human) energy" (9). Labeling him "an evangelist for modern romanticism" (10), they believe that the imaginative connection between the human and nonhuman realms becomes possible through constant pursuit, the willful search for its visions by what Lieberman (1967) calls a "worldly mystic" (513). For example, "Sleeping Out at Easter" depicts a speaker who intuits Nature's "compelling inner rhythms" (11) through his "personal regeneration ritual" (10). The italicized stanzas in the poem suggest a larger, oracular consciousness whose incantatory effects also lull the reader into the same mystical communion. Rituals in each of the four titled sections seek this larger, cosmic interplay. In poems like "The Signs," "The Call," "The Game," and "The String," the persona attempts to establish family connections, the last of these using ritual string tricks like "Cradle of Cat, the Foot of a Crow" to "bring my brother to myself." "The Wedding," a war poem, reveals the airmen's practice of making artifacts that constitute "symbols of and for themselves" (15). "Trees and Cattle" and "The Other" use ritual to confront death, often resulting in "his almost evangelical dislocation of normal sensual and intellectual conditions" (18) in order to establish a mandatory condition of wholeness. Calhoun and Hill, however, find the "Love" section only "a modest culmination" (19) of the unions achieved elsewhere in the book, primarily because the images are conventional and lack daring, connotative associations. The best of these, "Into the Stone," where the moon assumes Platonic implications to suggest an escape to an ideal realm, depicts Dickey's idea that human love resembles the mystical union an individual can attain in Nature.

Bloom (1985) opposes the pervasive critical view of Dickey as a poet of otherness, preferring instead to view him as a modern Emerson who heroically celebrates the self that "demands victory and disdains even great defeats" (63). Dickey is one of "the bards of divination" (63) from whom poetry first originated and whose willful vitality necessitated "a literal immortality for themselves as poets" (63). Not unlike Oates (1974), Bloom concludes that Dickey's poetry reveals the poet's progressive recognition of his own mortality, but he believes that the origin of his poetic quest lies in his guilt for being a substitute for his dead brother, a Freudian interpretation of *Into the Stone* that sees the otherness Dickey ultimately desires as an incarnation of the god Apollo. Bloom's specific focus is "The Other," where Dickey's effort to incarnate himself, to develop most fully his poetic character, becomes clouded by this early sense of guilt, or what he calls in the poem "my lust of self." Citing the poem's "striking dualism" (65), Bloom argues that "The Other" shows Dickey's need to become "his brother, or Apollo, or 'the Other'" (65) despite his egocentricity, a conflict that produces a permanent guilt. Dickey's particular mythology, in other words, serves from the beginning to present to himself the struggle of the "strength-haunted body" of a "rack-ribbed child" to achieve Herculean dimension. The truth of this confrontation becomes changed in the poem to a trope, the child's aspirations toward becoming Apollo or poetry itself.

Dickey states that he wrote *Drowning With Others* while he worked in advertising and that its creation arose from "the traumatic and blood-letting kinds of circumstances in which you're expected to be working full-time for business, but you're actually doing 'your own thing' part of the time" (*Self-Interviews* 101). Asserting that "I was selling my soul to the devil all day and trying to buy it back at night" (44), he concludes, "This makes you feel guilty" (101). One of the earliest critics to comment on Dickey, Nemerov (1963) primarily surveys the style and content of *Drowning With Others* and notes Dickey's use of three-beat lines, a technique providing a definite but not coercive form which allows flexibility and variation. As long as he does not overburden the anapest by insistent rhyming, the poems succeed, as in "The Summons," but when Dickey indulges in rhyme, as in "The Island," the procedure falters badly. Nemerov also faults the tendency to mystify all aspects of an experience, a forced use of language which results in the words functioning only to create atmosphere, as when Dickey writes in "The Owl King": "A perfect, irrelevant music / In which we profoundly moved." Rather than causing the reader to participate in the experience, this inclination and another quality, the overuse of participles to imply continuous action, merely call attention to themselves as poetic devices. The poems suggest a movement down the evolutionary scale of life, while the power to perceive the world as relation belongs both to the poet and some other, an idea that anticipates Weatherby (1966). Among these connections, Nemerov observes certain persistently dramatized familial relationships—the child to his father, and one "more autobiographical" (102), that of the poet to a brother who died before his own birth. Later critics such as Calhoun and Hill (1983) and Bloom (1985) stress the guilt derived from his older brother's death. Yet such a perspective owes largely to Dickey's own commentary in *Self-Interviews* when, discussing "The String," he states:

I *did* gather by implication and hints of family relatives that my mother, an invalid with angina pectoris, would not have dared to have another child if Gene had lived. I was the child who was born as a result of this situation. And I always felt a sense of guilt that my birth depended on my brother's death. (89)

Lacking the poet's admission, Nemerov simply assumes that the persona in the early poems is Dickey himself.

Bly (1964) sees this initial interest in the dead becoming a concern with kingship in *Drowning With Others* and cites "The Scratch" ("I will dream of a crown till I do"), "Dover: Believing in Kings," and "The Owl King" as examples. Kingship, moreover, frequently resides in animals; the poet enters them like "a new set of clothes" (46). As a consequence, divinity and the animal world often mix ("The Heaven of Animals" and "The Rib") with no regard for the character of the persona. After a spiritual transformation, the speaker usually falls back into a lower world from the angelic, a descent bypassing the human despite what Bly considers "a curious narcissism" (52).

Korgen (1963) detects in *Drowning With Others* a similar fullness of presentation centering on Dickey or his interests. The poems principally concern animals, family, and the poet himself or how often the poet is alone, either in a tree house, in woods or fog, or in a house of sleeping people. Often Dickey or the speaker locates himself "at the center of the world, or perhaps all creation" (489). Rarely does another character intrude either upon his discovery of self, the external world around him, or that world as it is psychically conceived. Certain poetic statements become intensely personal, as in "The Owl King" when Dickey writes, "Come, son, and find me here, / in love with the sound of my voice." One consequently senses a "Romantic ego" (489), an observation that anticipates Gregor's (1975) tribute to Dickey as an American romantic. Also, like Ramsey (1973), Korgen faults the rhyme, calling it "clumsy" (489) and citing particularly "The Island." However, Dickey's close observations and his ability to present these with rich, connotative images offset this failure. His description seems to "reach for meanings which cannot be located" (489). Moreover, since Dickey neither utilizes a rhyme pattern to identify stanzas nor prevents the stanzas themselves from breaking arbitrarily in the middle of sentences, form itself becomes an illusion with merely the appearance of logic, governed only by line count. Yet the poetic manner reflects the matter, for many of the poems in *Drowning With Others* deal with illusions or magic, as in "The Owl King." These poems manifest "a deep and abiding compassion" (490), a sympathy for animals, the dead and dying, and the outcast that constitutes a belief in "ancient faiths" (491).

Howard (1966) believes that *Drowning With Others* depicts the poet's initial advances into the world, his tentative abandonment of the processes and forms in *Into the Stone* and his embrace of "particular presences" (420) without the "explicit ceremony" (425) previously required. While "Inside the River," with its Heraclitean emphasis on flux and motion, merely implies Dickey's eventual release, "Dover: Believing in Kings" presents the experiences of life actually taking hold. Here, mythic concerns of inheritance and dispossession yield to the poet's departure in his car with his family to pursue their personal lives. Hodge (1985) essentially agrees, viewing the poem as "a mind trying to identify itself" (17) by distinguishing the elements of its personality from among the confusion of genes and heredity. The volume vividly reveals a tension between "the longed-for ritual and the lived reality, or the stress between an inherited ceremony and an unmediated response" (422). Unlike *Into the Stone*, moreover, the liturgy enlarges to approach illumination as the speaker struggles within his limited experience to discover the spiritual. He "*earns* rather than merely surrenders to the inescapable leap into spirit" (424). However, this emerging focus on immediate, particular concerns worries Kennedy (1962), who, after recognizing the personal themes of family, childhood, and nature, together with the poet's own perceptions, notes a danger—"a certain expectedness of diction" (4) involving words like "air," "water," "fire," and "moon."

Like Howard, Oates (1974) discerns in *Drowning With Others* a "more dramatic sense of self" (104). Poems like "The Lifeguard," "A Dog Sleeping on My Feet," and "The Movement of Fish" are concerned with the poet's own memories and perceptions. Yet other poems such as "The Heaven of Animals" and "The Owl King" remain strictly "poetic constructions" (105) where larger forces are restrained if not benevolent. Dickey simply accepts the transcendent vision, acquiescing to the "unearthly simplicity" (106) with no danger to himself. Baughman (1985), however, perceives a different dichotomy in Dickey's second volume. Exploring the condition of the dead, the speakers find themselves suspended between an underworld ("The Island" and "Between Two Prisoners") and a heaven where animals kill or are killed endlessly ("The Heaven of Animals"). With such literal or figurative death on the one hand and perfection on the other, any effort by the personae to achieve in their present existence a heightened life of vision, what Baughman calls a "kingly, angel-like stature" (9), simply results in failure ("The Owl King") or guilt ("The Lifeguard"). Moreover, to succeed in identifying with the dead world would mean destruction of the self. Only "In the Tree House at Night" offers the poet safety, a balance between the living and the dead or what Baughman sees as "a momentary, rather precarious barrier" (40) against entropy where ambiguity characterizes existence. After Dickey's effort in *Into the Stone* to confront and question otherness, *Drowning With Others* depicts his re-ordering of understanding, a larger knowledge of life as he now attempts to accommodate death.

Calhoun and Hill (1983) perceive Dickey's second volume as less Platonic and more Aristotelian than the first, with the later work emphasizing duality even while it extends the themes announced in *Into the Stone*. Social unity emerges as the poet's principal consideration because "the familiar guilt motif is made a social affair" (25). The title poem serves to "pluralize" (36) the figure of Dickey's dead brother, and while he appears in "In the Tree House at Night" and "Armor," other poems concern the father-child relationship, including "The Owl King," "Dover: Believing in Kings," "To His Children in Darkness," "The Hospital Window," "The Magus," "Antipolis," and "Facing Africa." Calhoun and Hill view this extension of concern as "a broadening, if not a maturing, of the poet's concerns" (29). In addition to suggesting a human fellowship, *Drowning With Others* merges the meaning of survivorship with Nature ("The Owl King") to imply that physical things possess an inherent meaning that can be learned. Nature's aspects, therefore, are not fictions, not the mere perceptions of human observers, though they occasionally fail to yield comfort, as in "The Lifeguard." Animals in this volume now become signs or symbols as Dickey's increasing use of memorable images begins to hint at the darkness behind appearances and the need for transcendence ("The Movement of Fish," "The Heaven of Animals," and "Fog Envelops the Animals"). Vulnerability requires the personae to search outward ("For the Nightly Ascent of the Hunter Orion over a Forest Clearing") and inward ("A Screened Porch in the Country"). "The Change" continues Dickey's interest in "the primordial essence of all natural things" (51). Behind the human search for transcendent meaning lies the poetic imagination, and "Autumn" and "In the Mountain Tent" underscore the awareness of mortality and the effort to discern the powers behind the world, as in the latter poem where Dickey writes of "the thought-out leaves of the wood."

Critics generally agree that *Helmets* constitutes the best volume in Dickey's early motion. Kennedy (1964) considers the book his most poetically advanced, one rich in "relentless intelligence" (5), and Donoghue (1964) views it as distinctly American, presenting "images of survival" (275) that offer the continuing possibility of "rising to local occasions, American occasions of insight" (275). Dickey insists upon a faithful presentation of human existence because he "prepares hopeless things for miracles" (275). While Bornhouser (1965) believes *Helmets* offers clearly revealed themes, he faults the arbitrary "spacial isolation" (150) in the poems and Dickey's hypnotic overuse of anapests that do not accommodate "natural speech rhythms" (150), both criticisms no longer valid in his central motion. Howard (1966) declares that *Helmets* confirms Dickey as "the telluric maker Wallace Stevens had called for" (425). The volume still suggests a concern with process, but the poem itself, not some magical control over nature, becomes the reward, and the poet becomes "a man speaking to himself, for others" (425), rather than a "necromancer" (425). Dickey's interest here lies with confronting his essential humanity, the naked self. For example, in "Drinking from a Helmet," the helmet becomes a possession not of some questing knight but one simply picked up from a dead G.I. out of which he drinks water. It conceals against some other and also protects against the rhythms and energies of the physical world. The poem therefore extends an image from *Into the Stone* ("The Signs") and *Drowning With Others* ("Armour") to reflect the movement in Dickey's poetry toward seeing the individual without mythic shroud. Similarly, "The Dusk of Horses" broadens "The Heaven of Animals" and "Listening to Foxhounds," while "At Darien Bridge" develops "Near Darien," where instead of an enchanted ground perceived or experienced as mystery, the site is objectively presented as a place built by convicts.

Howard (1966) sees *Helmets* as depicting Dickey's poetic judgment of the physical world by imposing justice on it. Like Donoghue (1964), he discerns "a kind of morality" (428) derived from particular occasions, as in "On the Coosawattee" where the speaker, sensing the violation of the natural order, says, "We believed ourselves doomed / And the planet corrupted forever." Nature attempts "to raise / Us from the sleep of the yet-to-be-drowned." The volume still employs ritual, but Howard believes it is not so much given as invented, an observation underscored by Dickey's abandonment of previous metrical measures and stanzaic forms. Though earlier rhythms remain, "the transformation of ritual into romance" (428) necessitates a metamorphosis of poetic style so that language more closely approaches consciousness. Like Howard, Oates (1974) discerns a new motion in *Helmets*, one that reveals not a focus on unities and correspondences in nature but "a new sense of exploration into an 'otherness'" (109). Dickey demystifies past thematic concerns to offer a more realistic examination where total acceptance now becomes contrasted with human suffering. "Cherrylog Road," for example, constitutes the first of this new type of poem, at once "nostalgic and comic" (110), where love, previously so mysterious and removed, is unglamorized. Names and places are given, and the narrator leaves on a motorcycle humorously presented: "Like the soul of the junkyard / Restored, a bicycle fleshed / With power." The "life-affirming magic" (113) still exists, but as "Drinking from a Helmet" suggests, it occurs as a consequence of another human being. Martz (1973) agrees that Dickey's previous sense of joyous affirmation has become tempered by a knowledge of anguish and despair, declaring that "Cherrylog Road" concludes with "a paradox of meaningless being" (81). Directed by the experience itself, the speaker remains forever trapped by both joy and misery ("Wild to be wreckage forever"), and the poet seems "torn apart by his own metaphor" (82). At best, the poem becomes for Dickey "an act of love" (83).

Baughman (1983) believes that *Helmets* distinguishes itself from the two earlier volumes because Dickey has found in his central image a means to advance control over his survivor's guilt. The helmet in "Drinking from a Helmet" simultaneously allows for "a reordering knowledge" (9) concerning combat death and a method of communication with those who are not casualties of war. In "Approaching Prayer," for example, the persona achieves illumination into both his own and his father's lives, and in "The Scarred Girl," he discovers an appreciation of inner beauty. Other poems reveal him connecting with Nature ("Springer Mountain") and experiencing love's enhancing power ("Cherrylog Road"). The helmet image assists the poet "both in concealing himself from death and guilt, and in approaching their mysteries" (10). By reordering his understanding, Dickey achieves a previously unknown sense of responsibility, even if the perceptions he gains sometimes serve to terrify rather than provide him a sense of glory, as in "The Ice Skin" and "Kudzu."

Unlike other critics, Calhoun and Hill (1983) place *Helmets* in Dickey's middle phase (54). About this volume Dickey states in *Self-Interviews*:

> The hunting theme took on a much greater importance, and I wanted
> to get back to the war theme in a way which had nothing to do with
> flying.... I wrote about the war from the standpoint of the infantry
> where you have a much closer intimacy with what happens to the
> *people* in a war. (124)

The assertion reflects the poet's larger social awareness, a more humanly
encompassing perspective. Few poems, however, confront hunting, and only
three poems focus on war, leading Calhoun and Hill to assert that, properly
speaking, these provide subject matter while "the theme of transcendence"
(54) dominates the volume. This transcendence is sometimes deliberately
sought ("On the Coosawattee," "Winter Trout," and "In the Marble
Quarry"). Even "Springer Mountain" presents a speaker consciously seeking
communion by nakedly chasing a deer in winter woods, all in an effort to
"'ritualize' his natural self" (57). Sometimes the enlightenment occurs
unexpectedly, unsought and unsolicited, as in "Chenille" and "Kudzu."
Finally, the personae are infrequently possessed, mystically violated by some
other, as in "Approaching Prayer" and "The Being."

    While not using the word "transcendence," Bloom (1985) sees *Helmets* as
"a struggle against facticity" (74), where Dickey's major preoccupations
move toward being satisfied. Particularly in "Drinking from a Helmet," the
speaker divines meaning by discovering "the right cover of otherness" (75)
and simultaneously finds salvation from death by achieving "the magic body
of the poet" (75). Discovering in the final lines "the magic of substitution"
(78), he unites himself with the poet's essential self: "And tell him where I
had stood, / What poured, what spilled, what swallowed: / And tell him I
was the man." The poetic character becomes, then, not only empirical and
ontological but also "a divine other" (78).

2: *Buckdancer's Choice* and *Poems 1957-1967*

LIKE HIS PREVIOUS VOLUMES, Dickey divides *Buckdancer's Choice* (1965) into four sections; unlike them, however, the first and last of these divisions consist only of one long poem, "The Firebombing" and "Slave Quarters," respectively. These two poems, along with "The Fiend," have provoked the most critical commentary because they exhibit what Dickey calls a "block format" ("Preface," *The Central Motion* v) where the reader physically confronts a wall of words, as it were, that forces him to climb down the page. They also utilize a "split line" technique (*Babel to Byzantium* 290), which fragments the poetic line by grouping clusters of words and phrases. The reader jumps from one idea to another, the spaces serving as transitional devices, or interstices in the wall, to reflect either the way the mind itself associates or the pauses in the persona's speaking voice. This stylistic innovation, so different from Dickey's early motion, signaled a shift in poetic direction and immediately attracted critical examination, particularly when the volume won first the Melville Cane Award and then the National Book Award.

Dickey became restless with the rhythmical and halluncinatory method as well as with narrative elements; after three volumes, they seemed like another set of literary conventions. His experimentation led to what he labels the "open poem" (*Babel to Byzantium* 290), a form whose compulsiveness would preclude the reader from passing a literary judgment and instead allow him simply to experience the poem with direct immediacy. Critics noted not only the technical innovation but also a larger, social awareness depicted in language suggesting strain and violence. While some considered the volume decidedly different from his earlier works, others viewed it as a culmination of his themes and techniques. Joseph Bennett (1966) discerns the uniqueness of *Buckdancer's Choice*, declaring that Dickey's previous volumes reveal only the development of a particular style and subject matter. These abilities now become clearly focused and show "a lensing of the totality of being into a kind of carefully separated madness" (10). In particular, the utilization of a "gap-device" (10) within single lines provides an impulsive movement and what Bennett calls an "exploded narrative" (10), citing "The Firebombing" specifically. Glancy (1971) suggests that while *Buckdancer's Choice* shares with the early volumes similar themes of love, death, and transcendence, it also reveals a change in the persona. Previously, the figure was "weakly autobiographical" (26) and endeavored to lose his self in some larger other, usually nature. Now, however, the persona obtains insight or revelation as a result of another's experience, which allows the poet to become, as he writes in the title poem, "nearly risen" over the limitations of his physical condition. The method extends reality to celebrate the "human family" (30) in its largest sense. Howard (1966) believes Dickey's fourth book distinctive because it displays "the transformation from ritual into romance" (480). The incantatory early poems now give way to brutal, disjointed actions that, while performed and even occasionally celebrated, are then discarded. While "Fox Blood" and "War Wound" suggest the previous magical world, a realm of "available correspondences" (481) where things assume the qualities of some other, Dickey for the most part abandons his interest in a return to ideal forms and focuses instead on "a linear movement within time" (481). He realizes that the individual personality dies, and this pervasive fear of extinction dominates the volume. Like Bennett (1966), Howard believes *Buckdancer's Choice* reveals a sense of obsession, madness, and excess, but declares that these constitute the penalty of "the historical imagination" (481). Its reward is a more conscious awareness of others now explicitly presented, an observation which anticipates Glancy's (1971) view that revelation is obtained vicariously.

Critics recognize the relationship between the precarious perspective offered by these poems and their style; manner reflects matter. The new uncertainty about one's existence, the realization of mortality and a hoped-for regeneration rather than a willed return, demands a new metric. Howard suggests that the blank spacing between words indicates "a separateness in the writer's experience" (482). Dickey deliberately contrasts long lines with ones truncated to reveal both an awareness of death and the need to believe not in larger-than-life figures like kings, as in the early volumes, but in ordinary individuals like himself. Davison (1967) sees this openness in Dickey's narrative and his exploitation of its possibilities as reflecting "a liberation of violence" (120). While this freedom implies the previous suppression of both personal memories and poetic themes, the new rhythms render past experiences concerning war and aerial combat with more presentational immediacy. Additionally, the poet now juxtaposes the reality of his past with that of the present. These new elements in Dickey's poetry distinguish his "maturity" (120) from the early work. Gregor (1973) similarly discerns in *Buckdancer's Choice* Dickey's "energy" (78), a feature he believes distinctly American, which the poet uses to achieve a spiritual end and which reflects his own personal vitality. To control this energy, he creates a style appropriate to restraining and directing this power, specifically the use of short phrases that deliver a distinct staccato beat within long, free-flowing lines (78). Whatever Dickey's subject matter, his work remains essentially affirmative (79), a part of the romantic and visionary tradition that confronts "the unchanging human dilemma" (79). Davison's "violence" and Gregor's "energy" differ only in semantics. Both see the extension of themes and a new metric, though the former considers this representative of Dickey's central motion while the latter's principal focus is not so much on any developmental stage as his essential sense of American affirmation.

Oates (1974) views the new poetry as decidedly more serious and pessimistic than the earlier volumes; it addresses more directly and brutally the physical conditions of this life. Whereas even the ruthless execution earlier in "The Performance" possesses a "mystical placidity" (113), actions are now bluntly examined and emotionally charged as Dickey confronts modern existence without "the sustaining rituals of Being" (113). Baughman (1985) more specifically details this change. Declaring that Buckdancer's *Choice* shows Dickey's full poetic maturity, he believes that the new openness in form, so discernibly longer and less concentrated, suggests a conscious abandonment of the protective or concealing masks used in *Helmets*, thereby enabling the poet to face the questions that have confronted him throughout his work. Moreover, Dickey presents all his major thematic concerns. In "The Firebombing," for example, he asks whether his aerial combat missions in the Second World War necessitate his seeking either absolution or solace, and though the answer never arrives, that he raises the issue reveals his attempt to move "from self-laceration toward protective renewal" (63). The family poems center on the relationship between mother and child, which has provided him life even as it has also engendered his guilt at being alive. "Slave Quarters," Dickey's most important social poem, examines the morality underlying the slave-master relationship, specifically its elements of love and hate that constitute so much a part of the poet's Southern history. One of Dickey's love poems, "The Fiend," dramatically confronts the strangely heightened passion of a voyeur. Dickey also returns to nature in "The Shark's Parlor" to depict how a boy's climactic victory over a shark continues to haunt him even though it brought him youthful glory. In cataloguing these works, Baughman declares that Dickey openly faces "the ambiguities caught in survivor's guilt" (63) and accepts no simple answers for complex modern concerns.

Calhoun and Hill (1983) examine *Buckdancer's Choice* by critiquing its respective sections and briefly comparing them to *Helmets*, although unlike Baughman (1985), they offer no comprehensive overview of the volume. Whereas *Helmets* departs from the concern with family that preoccupies Dickey's first two books, *Buckdancer's Choice* returns to it with a clearer focus and more compassion than in the previous volumes. Two poems concern his mother ("Buckdancer's Choice" and "Angina"), one his father and mother together ("The Celebration"), and two others ("The Second Sleep" and "The Aura") are grouped under a collective title, "Fathers and Sons." Four of these five poems depict the demise of a family member; only "The Celebration" appropriately focuses on the living. The emphasis on hunting that Dickey believes is in *Helmets* appears much more fully in this new book. While the former includes nature imagery primarily vegetative ("Kudzu"), the latter presents three poems concerning animate life at its most vicious. Dickey scrutinizes the darker side of nature in "Pursuit from Under," "Reincarnation," and "The Shark's Parlor," which concern a killer whale, a rattlesnake, and a hammerhead shark, respectively, to show that "transcendence is not always a thing of joy" (66). This sinister view of the physical world transforms Dickey's depiction of hunting to reveal a mindless, undiminished force capable of awesome terror. His sexual poems also contain an aspect of hunting. In "The Fiend," for example, he shows "passion itself to be fearsome" (70), and while the voyeur offers no sense of remorse for his actions, the theme of guilt appears in "The Firebombing" and "Slave Quarters" and assumes a larger, more social response than Dickey earlier revealed.

Unlike other critics, Strange (1965-66) sees *Buckdancer's Choice* as displaying two recognizably modern sets of poems. Rather than a division according to thematic concerns, Strange discerns poems that are dreams either in fact or technique and another set whose basis is memory, poems that are remembered. So integral is this scheme to the book that in "Fathers and Sons" Dickey combines two poems, one depicting a young boy asleep and dreaming while his father dies and another presenting a father overwhelmed by memories of his dead son. Other poems function similarly but link themselves to earlier volumes to suggest such a balance. "Pursuit from Under," for example, anticipates and joins "Sled Burial, Dream Ceremony," as does "Faces Once Seen" with "The Common Grave." The most striking poems in *Buckdancer's Choice* unite the elements of both dream and memory, such as "The Firebombing" and "The War Wound." Of the two categories, the dreams are the less successful because such transformations of men into beasts are "old hat" (34), though Strange acknowledges that Dickey masterfully uses "all the turns of a neo-Freudian rhetoric" (34). "The Celebration," in fact, constitutes so clinically correct a psychoanalytic poem that Dickey seems to be deliberately showing the need to move beyond "our time's craft of dreams" to demand "visions *of more than one's self*" (38). That the poet wishes to escape solipsism is revealed by a fullness of presentation of other people in *Buckdancer's Choice*, including generations of family, friends, an invalid teacher, a truck driver, a voyeur, a slave owner, and a pilot, all of which manifest Dickey's "appetite" (39), as he writes in "Mangham," for "Identities! Identities!" Because the title poem shows that time does indeed pass, Strange declares that "Buckdancer's Choice" represents "a perfect emblem of the act he would achieve" (42), a poetry of "prophecy" that reveals what was and what shall be.

Critics focus on the new metrical techniques of Dickey's central motion, particularly in the long poems like "The Firebombing" and "Slave Quarters." Lensing (1973) sees the less formal and psychically exaggerated narrations as apropos of Dickey's tendency to project ever more imaginative poems. Rather than continue an identification with animal life, he endeavors to create works concerned with passion and violence and which center specifically on sex and death. To accommodate this new direction, he uses fluid, open lines, often containing shorter lines within them, and sequences of participial and gerundive phrases to provide a sense of "free sweep" (173). Lieberman's (1968) examination, "Notes on James Dickey's Style," argues that the principal unit of metrical measure is "a breath unit (or breathing unit), as opposed to a grammatical unit" (60), while the sentence itself all but disappears. Because a sentence beginning or ending will sometimes "punctuate" (199) a large measure of the poem, the reader receives the impression of moving within "the extremities of a rather free-floating sentence" (60). The poem itself corresponds to "a welter of experience in flux" (60) because it maintains a continuous motion, incorporating more and more experience into it and resembling the technique of film. Breaks in verse paragraphing resemble shifts in perspective, a building up or slowing down of onrush. The technique enables Dickey to extend the boundaries of what the poet may possibly say, because enlarging the resources of language makes available deep sensibilities that lie beyond consciously willed and structured poetic forms.

Ramsey's (1973) metrically detailed analysis of Dickey's new poetry provides the fullest understanding not only of its complexity but also the success or failure of the technique. The shorter poems in *Buckdancer's Choice* reveal varied line lengths, usually of two- and four-stress verses, with "Sled Burial, Dream Ceremony" offerring the best example. Here Dickey's use of rising trimeter, a carry-over from his early motion, mingles with verses where pentameter dominates to offer a "counterpatterning" (182). Such variation is effective when the created rhythms reinforce the narrative, but often they serve to undermine it. Dickey's only other extensively used form, "the subdivided long-line free verse" (183), increasingly dominates the middle stage of his career, its central motion. Long-line free verse works well by "rhetorical and grammatical parallelism; by sweep; and by accumulation" (183), but if subdivided, it risks puzzling the reader unless both levels of this division remain distinct. Otherwise, the result is only a "jerky, overstressed, over-paused prose" (183). Dickey's use of this form in "The Shark's Parlor" is problematic for while the action powerfully exhibits a heroic hunt that leads to manhood, the meter "adds little and detracts much" (184). The long verses lack any consistent principle that might support the narrative, which though related straightforwardly as a memory, is "presumably a nightmare or partially sur-natural imaginings" (184). Ramsey baldly asserts that any effort to use "a rhetorical punctuation or spacing" (184) to induce a particular reader response is "grossly inadequate" (184-85). When read as spaced, "The Shark's Parlor" yields the sense of "a hysterical sort of force" (185), but such a method quickly becomes detrimental. In "The Birthday Dream" this spacing simply "crudens" (185) the reading, though in "The Fiend" the technique works best because the gaps either signify natural speech pauses or provide valid emphasis.

Because of their length, the new metrical structure they exhibit, and their controversial subject matter, "The Firebombing," "Slave Quarters," and "The Fiend" merit particular critical focus. Dickey himself states in *Self-Interviews* that "The Firebombing" depicts "a very complex state of mind" (137), the speaker's inability to feel guilt as a consequence of his participation in aerial warfare when he is entitled, as a result of his actions, to such feelings. Having returned to a life of domestic inconsequence, the persona nevertheless yearns for combat and the excitement it afforded him. Of such men, Dickey declares, "The greatness is not only in an ideological sense, but exists also because millions of people are involved in the event" (138). No longer able to enter such a complex state, he concludes, "They wouldn't be heroes or even potential heroes then; they would only be ordinary human beings" (138). Initial reviews offerred only brief analyses of the poem and either failed to discern the guilt motif or else treated it sparingly. Duncan (1964) states that the firebomber himself possesses no "creative freedom" (133) and therefore must relive the napalm, "anti-morale" raids demanded by his fantasy, insulated by the orders delivered from military command. The poem, which presents this fantasy, is itself an imaginative creation where both the character and the modern world's conveniences are routinely assumed by the poet whose mind is "sophisticated to their advertised values" (132). While Duncan presupposes a possible autobiographical connection and the poet's inability to control the fantasy he creates, Lieberman (1967) declares that Dickey deliberately places the personae of his long poems in predicaments of modern American life that create "an aura of grave moral jeopardy" (513), situations in which the Self is psychologically divided and incapable of establishing life-sustaining connections with the world because of their "moral guilt" (513). Materialism blocks this struggle to achieve "the free interchange of spirit between being and being" (514). Bly (1967) complains that "The Firebombing" fails to criticize the American tendency to bomb Asians with incendiaries and asserts that Dickey, dwelling on the excitement derived by re-experiencing the bombing mission, feels no personal suffering himself. The poem's message is that "military brutality is right" (75). Bly's critique, partly an *ad hominem* attack on what he considers is the poet's support of the Viet Nam war when he categorically believes all writers should oppose it, concludes by charging that Dickey increasingly "takes his life and laminates poetry onto it" (78). Anticipating Bowers's view that Dickey promotes himself in order to sell his poetry, Bly laments Dickey's "decision" to make poetry a "'career'" (79), a choice resulting in the "abrupt decline" (79) of his work.

Lieberman ("The Deepening of Being" 1968) also notes the "strange joy" (1) that constitutes part of Dickey's poetic vision and suggests that its movement into social and political issues creates "moments of ecstasy" (1) that threaten to overwhelm the agony which is the poem's central concern. "The Firebombing" culminates a sequence of war poems that includes "The Performance," "The Jewel," and "Drinking from a Helmet," and presents two "beings" (5) who, though simultaneously in conflict, are nevertheless removed from each other. One is lost in time, while the other battles a moral stupor, and Dickey's central strategy becomes their confrontation in an effort to obtain a catharsis. What he says, however, at the poem's conclusion ("Absolution? Sentence? No matter; / The thing itself is in that.") is that art fails to achieve this expiation because, in the persona's hands, "art itself is an unclean instrument" (5). Whatever feelings of guilt arise from his remembrance of the event are subverted by those of joy and power encountered during the mission. If the poem sincerely attempts to present

Dickey's own efforts at moral expiation by again placing himself in the blue light of the "glass treasure-hole" and by providing his persona with the identical "aesthetic contemplation" as the aircraft flies over "the *heart* of the fire," then his subsequent excitement reveals that the poet becomes "trapped in the tools of his art" (6). The failure of Dickey's explicitly acknowledged goal suggests that what is not contained in "the thing itself" is simply incapable of being poetically presented. Art miscarries in its effort to achieve for the speaker a final understanding of his combat experiences.

Oates (1974) does not discuss the poem as an imaginative act but like Howard (1966) sees Dickey's emerging self-consciousness about his own mortality. In an essay titled "The Son, the Cave, and the Burning Bush," first published in Carroll's *The Young American Poets* (1968), Dickey writes of this concern:

> The aging process almost always brings to the poet the secret conviction that he has settled for far too little, that he has paid too much attention to the "limitations" that his contemporaries have assured him he has, as well as to literary tradition and the past.... The nearer he gets to his end the more he yearns for the cave: for a wild, shaggy, all-out, all-involving way of speaking where language and he (or, now, someone: some new poet) engage each other at primitive levels, on ground where the issues are not those of literary fashion but are quite literally those of life and death. (67)

Anxiety about one's mortality anticipates *The Eye-Beaters, Blood, Victory, Madness, Buckhead and Mercy* (1970) and strongly dominates the poetic narrative of "The Firebombing." Despite the poem's epigraph from Job ("Or hast thou an arm like God?"), the persona's detachment, his utter removal from the bombing's effects, is not godly but suggests despair. Declaring that "The Firebombing" constitutes "the central poem of his work" (113), Oates focuses on the speaker's state of being and the blunt and brutal way Dickey confronts life and death without the techniques of ritual that earlier sustained him. The unresolved ending owes to the fact that no reconciliation is possible for "this poetry of anguished Becoming" (118). The poet cannot harmonize what he is with what he was, and the lack of any possible reconciliation necessitates an "aesthetic-denying open form" (118).

The controversy ignited by Bly's (1967) attack on Dickey, together with their decade-long feud, first initiated and then sustained interest in "The Firebombing." Eventually a reassessment began. Berke (1981), for example, states that the poem's "overt motive" (115) is survival because power, while sometimes corrupt, is a reality and mandatory to achieve high goals. Language, moreover, is itself power and remains for most poets the principal means of attaining their ends. Both Ross Bennett (1980) and Baughman (1983) scrutinize the poem more closely than the initial critical responses, the first through specific textual analysis, which Bly never attempts, and the latter by placing the poem within the context of Dickey's war poetry. Bennett contends that the poem's subject is not the expiation of guilt as Lieberman (1967) argues but rather "the redemptive power of memory" (433). Bly incorrectly suggests that there is no persona in "The Firebombing" and that Dickey and his speaker are identical. However, more than one persona may exist because tone and imagery in those sections where the speaker describes his present life or comments on his past memories remain essentially different from those in which he actually re-creates the firebombing raid. They represent "two different voices, two different characters, dual protagonists in an interior drama" (431). The poet himself is both involved in this "process of personal self-discovery" (432) and yet detached from it as "an autonomous, self-contained work of art" (432). Therefore, the narrator is not necessarily synonymous with Dickey himself. Moreover, the firebomber is an imaginative re-creation, an invention, the efficacy of which becomes the poem's essential focus. Dickey examines memory's ability not merely to distort the reality perceived by the senses but to release previously unknown aspects of one's self. The sympathetic imagination here fails to effect such knowledge because "the intrusion of distorting art perspectives may inhibit true vision" (443). Rather than discovering the reality of what happened, the imagination leads into "a world of illusion" (443). Dickey's redemptive use of illusion in early poems to sustain and enhance now becomes perilously close to delusion, as when the speaker comments, "It is this detachment, / The honored aesthetic evil, / The greatest sense of power in one's life / That must be shed in bars, or by whatever / Means...." The statement constitutes for Bennett "an impassioned denunciation of a flawed art, of a dehumanized imagination that has lost contact with reality" (444). Yet while the quest for a sympathetic knowledge fails, the poem succeeds because it communicates "the process of that failure" (448).

Baughman (1983) sees Dickey's continued interest in war as suggesting a personal need to clarify the conflict's fundamental meaning, its influences on how he views both his life and his art. Beginning with "The Jewel," he has poetically questioned his encounter with death. After "Drinking from a Helmet," the poet moved "from 'confrontation' to 'reordering'" (44), dramatizing his own conflicts rather than depending upon others as "agents for his own self-exploration" (44). "The Firebombing" culminates his efforts at understanding because the poem allows him to examine the complexity of emotions associated with his personal involvement. What distinguishes it is Dickey's ability to identify simultaneously with his role of executioner and with his victims, a union that brings his "spiritual rebirth" (44) by providing self-illumination. The speaker faces the terrifying ambiguities his role assigned him, and he accepts them.

"Slave Quarters," another poem where guilt dominates but which involves a condition of love rather than war, also precipitated intense critical commentary when *Buckdancer's Choice* appeared. Friedman (1966), having labeled "The Firebombing" only as a poem "lost in disjunction, hallucinatory and kaleidoscopic imagery, and the lack of progression and climax" (63), nevertheless sees "Slave Quarters" as displaying "Dionysiac ecstasy" (65) but in a "demonic context" (66). Dickey's poetic question, "How to take on the guilt / of Slavers?" reveals the conflict between "unacknowledged sensuality and the misery it nonetheless creates" (66), an interpretation shared by Kirschten (1985), who sees in the poem Dickey's sense of "the monstrous" (80) and the "subordination to the laws of nature" (164). Bly's (1967) view that art must provide atonement necessitates his condemning "Slave Quarters" not only because the poem glorifies power and its use but also because it artistically decorates ugly Southern prejudice and contributes to stereotyping of blacks. Mills (1968) sympathizes with such criticism, declaring that the poem employs a speaker whose principal desire is the realization of his own perverted fantasies through a "warped masculine sexual power" (240). As in "The Firebombing," Dickey displays an "obsession" (240) with the willed imposition of power while simultaneously remaining oblivious to its effect. Lieberman (1967), however, discerns no such personal or political motive on Dickey's part. "Slave Quarters" shows only that "materialism" (513), as represented by the cultural stereotyping of racial occupations, precludes the speaker's uniting with the world. Niflis (1972) assumes a middle position, asserting that when Dickey speaks of "my imagining loins," he identifies himself as his own persona, but the poem's focus is the conflict between man's basic biological drives and the strictures imposed by society. Additionally, though he fails to go as far as Ross Bennett (1980) does with "The Firebombing" by suggesting the poem concerns the artistic process, Niflis does see "Slave Quarters" as exemplifying Dickey's commitment to imaginative work by confronting with language what has previously been thought but never well expressed.

In *Self-Interviews* Dickey clearly identifies his poetic intent regarding "Slave Quarters"—the exposure of Southern hypocrisy and the "renewal" (161) socially forbidden sex might sometimes have occasioned by stripping away the false and stultifying gentility characteristic of the plantation system. Moreover, the issue of a male offspring through forced, clandestine intercourse, a son who despite his paternity would be condemned to work the fields as a possession, would engender guilt because his father cannot acknowledge him. Closer critical commentary on "Slave Quarters" begins with Oates's (1974) discussion of the poem's eyesight imagery, a motif in Dickey's later poetry that complements "the mysterious grace of masculinity itself" (124). The loss of vision causes a corresponding denial of control, which may paradoxically produce a "glorious savagery" (124) but which may also facilitate a more sinister betrayal of one's expected sensibilities, as "Slave Quarters" shows. The poem addresses the many forms betrayal assumes, including that of others' eyes, as when Dickey writes: "It is to look once a day / Into an only / Son's brown, waiting, wholly possessed / Amazing eyes, and not / Acknowledge, but own." The poem's central concern is how one accepts the guilt one deserves. Calhoun and Hill (1983) agree but contend that the remorse from such deeds is clearly "a willful act of the imagination" (74), the main proof of which is the poem's final stanza where the speaker admits to his merely thinking out the situation. This artistic detachment enables Dickey to bring together not only the various senses of guilt but also the presence of the dead, the transcendence needed to effect a larger unity, and the limitations of the imagination. "Slave Quarters" seems strained because it attempts mentally to balance this large number of concerns; and though these do not coalesce, they nevertheless render the poem "a compendium of the major themes" (75) in the poet's middle period.

Baughman (1985) views the poem's principal motif not so much as guilt, though he recognizes Dickey's own acknowledgment of this theme, but rather as "a special kind of love" (68), one which contains an indifference that is itself a form of hate. Though the encounters between master and slave are described as "love," the owner's arrogance qualifies the emotion. His passion derives from the power over other human beings, and while the emotion itself is "good, alive" (70), the owner's abandonment of the black woman and their child produces profound guilt. As with "The Firebombing," the speaker bridges time by imaginatively fusing the past and present. However, Calhoun and Hill (1983) see such temporal manipulation within the same familial concern Dickey evidences in his early poems. Although the speaker's entrance into the historical past also puts him at the mercy of "the characters of his mind" (75), the necessity of maintaining the family structure transcends the expanse of historical perspective.

"The Fiend," the third of Dickey's long narratives in *Buckdancer's Choice*, has received less critical attention than either "The Firebombing" or "Slave Quarters" and is generally considered less successful. Davison (1967) notes that Dickey for the first time explores sexual deviance and, pointing to his "mature technique" and "dazzling" (121) characterization of a middle-aged voyeur, believes it equals these other poems in narrative progression and the movement backward and forward in time and space. However, Bowers (1985) states that Dickey's split-line form and the third-person point of view indicate not simply the poet's interest in narrative technique but also his general use of devices that involve the reader and thereby "sell the poem" (51). The narrator here intervenes between the poem's main character and the reader, thus eliminating the possibility of speech but raising the reader's interest in "the kind of internal conversations we all experience" (51). Bly (1967) also believes that Dickey deliberately manipulates the poem. The conclusion leaves the voyeur with "the light / Of a hundred windows gone wrong somewhere in his glasses / Where his knocked-off Panama hat was in his painfully vanishing hair." Yet it suggests also that he will knife to death the woman whose nakedness he has been unable to see. That Dickey only implies this tragedy rather than having the narrative depict it results from his realization that he might lose the *New Yorker* audience, where the poem originally appeared, should he be so explicit. Dickey consequently "didn't quite have the courage of his own sadism" (76). Mills (1968) faults not the motive but the poet's participation in an act from which he seems distant, showing little concern for the woman's fate. As in "The Firebombing," Dickey here exhibits total insensitivity to those who are the focus of his imaginative indulgence. Moreover, the depiction of a speaker whose private sexual delusions reveal warped masculine power and who determines to actualize his fantasies through violence exhibits "a sort of lyricism of the perverse" (240). Lieberman (1967), while similarly faulting Dickey's perceived indifference, states that "The Fiend" "lacks risk" because "the center of the poem's vision is too far from tragedy and believable danger" (518). While the voyeur is psychologically convincing, the poem does not convey the woman's ideal world extending to hold and transform the agony of the fiend.

Recent critics view the poem more favorably. Calhoun and Hill (1983), for example, point out that the voyeur's penetrating gaze idealizes the women he beholds and offers them "a curious protectiveness, a skewed paternalism" (71). Baughman (1985) considers the protagonist a mixture of good and evil. While the poem's title suggests society's conventional view of the Peeping Tom, his actions become "a source for love" (73). As the potential for violent death fuses with the possibility of a transforming love, the fiend bestows his gift: "He gives them all a first look that goes / On and on conferring immortality while it lasts." Baughman concludes that the poem examines moral extremes far removed from traditional romantic ideas by presenting "a complex vision of human passions and their potential" (75). Van Ness (1989) believes "The Fiend" examines "the positions of power" (8) from which both sexes view the other: the need of men to control events and the desire of women to demand attention. More specifically, the woman becomes an idealized figure capable of transforming the voyeur, a figure whose "movement can restore the green eyes / Of middle age looking renewed."

Though also written in a block format, "The Shark's Parlor" has not attracted much critical comment because of its shorter length and a subject matter less controversial than "The Firebombing" or "Slave Quarters." The poem concerns "a *rite de passage*, that is, growing up through some kind of traumatic experience" (*Self-Interviews* 146). Unlike the other block poems, the examination of two young men who drink beer for the first time and then attempt to catch a shark only indirectly involves a study of power. Dickey declares: "The necessity for kids, especially boys, to overmatch themselves, to take on more than they are qualified to handle, seems to me absolutely characteristic of male youth" (146). Kirschten (1988) applies to the poem Dickey's general principles of mysticism, Neoplatonism, romanticism, and primitivism. Calling "The Shark's Parlor" a comic poem "of redemption through victimage and ordeal" (8), he argues that the narrator's recollection of the events requires a syntactic representation that transcends memory to depict elements of the primal ritual. Dickey's intent "to force his agents *through* an extraordinarily detailed process" (198) results in line divisions, punctuation, and the accumulation of blood, sea, household, and swamp imagery that mix with the action to effect "the psychic transference of primal force from the shark to the boys" (198). Edwards (1991), stating that Kirschten's discussion of technique ignores "the harmony of the poem's various elements" (19), declares that other images suggest the persona's "recognition and acceptance of his own mortality" (21). The boys being simultaneously pulled in two directions, the relationship of the shark to the house, and the placement of specific numbers throughout the poem all reinforce the narrator's psychological progression from a loss of innocence to his recognition of "the ultimate consequence of his being human" (21). The acceptance of mortality at the conclusion of "The Shark's Parlor" finds the persona "Feeling more in two worlds than in one" because the ritual confirms his understanding of himself as spirit and body.

The publication of *Poems 1957-1967* initiated a general reassessment of Dickey's work. The volume opens with a new long poem, "May Day Sermon to the Women of Gilmer County, Georgia, by a Woman Preacher Leaving the Baptist Church," and includes portions of *Into the Stone, Drowning With Others*, and *Helmets*; all the poems in *Buckdancer's Choice*; and a new section titled "Falling." This last part Dickey published separately in 1981 as *Falling, May Day, and Other Poems*. Because *Poems 1957-1967* is Dickey's first collection of past work, critics use it not only to gauge his poetic development but also to detail his previously unexamined images or themes and to show how "Falling" and the other new poems reveal changes in attitude and technique. Meredith (1967), for example, notes the return of public utility to American poetry and suggests that Dickey's work belongs with that of Whitman, Masters, and Sandburg. Despite the tendency to allow his themes to wander into formlessness, he tries to discover the poetic shapes and forms that directly correspond to the testimony of the experience he relates, and while "Falling" does this, "May Day Sermon" does not. Instead, it is overly long and melodramatic. Morris (1969) condemns Dickey's consistent avoidance of standard verse patterns, stating that while his early poems observed a stanzaic form, the principle of stanza length remains unknown since rhyme and units of thought, image, and sound do not justify the regularity. Moreover, Dickey's later work is so loose as to allow "any dispersal, admit any discourse, follow any digression" (321). Other critics, however, like Landess (1975) and Mack Smith (1985), praise his poetic ingenuity. Landess states that Dickey depicts "the nature of modern secular society" (7) and offers traditional values regarding family, country, and God. Despite traditional critics who contend that Dickey's personal and "open" poems show a lack of "decorum and indirection" (5), the poet presents "broader historical implications" (12) through specific narrative situations without losing their essential human truth. Focusing on the poetic technique, Mack Smith insists that the narrative, rather than remaining only a cause-and-effect formula, becomes "the locus of struggle between the magical and literalist uses of language" (19). Consequently, a story is not a movement from place to place but a motion from one level of language to another, including the prophetic. Moreover, Dickey's resolution of this linguistic dichotomy often results in "narratives of a journey within" (21). What would have been changes in cause and effect become "shifts in voice" (21), variations of perspective that allow for the possibility of transcendence.

Corrington's (1968) appraisal argues the unique form, subject matter, and style of the poems in Dickey's first collection, with each poem standing distinct and yet interconnected with others chronologically before and after it. Insight and the imaginative capacity to define it both deepen and enlarge as one progressively examines the poetry. For example, "A Folk-Singer of the Thirties," so public in its vision of the country, becomes a "companion-piece" (23) to the more private "Falling," which depicts the same vision but now internalized. Metz (1979), however, declares that Dickey's volumes reveal consistent patterns of imagery, and that while form and style have changed, the subject matter stays the same. In particular, animals and children remain surrounded by "an aura of blessedness" (45). The variety of animals, occasionally imaginary but more often wild and domestic creatures, all exhibit "a fidelity to their role" (45), a fact most discernible in poems focusing on predator and prey. Poems involving children are less numerous but still depict this recurrent image, from that of Dickey's dead brother in "The String," to the small boy who returns in an illusion in "The Life-guard," and to Jane MacNaughton whose jumps, first at a dance and then later from a hotel window, continue to haunt the speaker in "The Leap." Metz believes the poems involving both children and animals, including "Walking on Water," "The Owl King," "The Shark's Parlor," and "The Sheep Child," are the most dramatically provocative.

Guillery (1970) discerns in the poems a search for an original response to water as symbol, a response that includes both the traditional associations of birth and fertility as well as the connotation of death by drowning and destruction by flood. Dickey combines water's dual roles, for example, in "Mary Sheffield," where the young woman's death fails to overwhelm the narrator with grief because he realizes she has absorbed the water's life-providing qualities to become eternal. Poems like "Walking on Water" and "The Lifeguard" allude to Christ's walking on water. Though the speaker in the latter does not effect his miracle and the drowned boy remains a child "Of water, water, water," a later poem, "Night Pool," shows the persona as "a successful savior" (133). Moreover, Dickey portrays water's ability to purify in "The Owl King," where the child passes through water to discern, "I am there, on the other side." Water is also a mystery in itself, imbued with "primal significance" (134), as in "The Vegetable King" and "Facing Africa," and "The Movement of Fish" reveals "a consciousness of evil" (135) within water. Dickey's most comprehensive understanding of water is in "Pursuit from Under." Where previously he displays in each poem one aspect of water as symbolic, here he depicts this element as "an ideal medium for harmonious understanding and fraternal communication" (135) because water is "the ultimate harmony" (135). Its very creation lies in numerous opposites. Tracing the growing understanding of Dickey's personae in poems involving water reveals that this element is simultaneously "the medium and the message" (137).

Haule (1979) examines Dickey's poems on the basis of closure—their ability not simply to end but to offer "a coherent expression of the whole"

(32). When the poet essentially eliminates meter and rhyme scheme, a poem's integrity should remain recognizably apparent owing to the absence of these familiar techniques. It is not that the last line becomes final, but that as a consequence of that line, the reader perceives the poem's unity. Dickey often ends his early works through refrain after allowing "an almost musical intonation" (34) to establish a poem's symmetry. The refrains become not merely a factual determination but a chanted statement of affirmation that, when combined to form a final stanza, suggest "the mystery of creation" (36) or "the message of indestructible life" (37). The early motion reveals both a tendency to avoid formal diction in favor of fragmentation and the decision not to close poems in the traditional sense. Rather, they conclude but do not end. In *Falling*, however, he moves more decidedly in favor of language whose form depends only on cadence and whose symbolic power resides in personal image. Rhythm is "conversational" (41), enjambment becomes debatable, and words are separated to enhance their importance. Moreover, Dickey breaks speech into its "natural units" (42) so that the poet and his persona blend.

Citing Dickey's own commentary in *Self-Interviews* that he remains a "born believer," Raymond Smith (1972) argues that the "capacity for belief" (259) dominates his poetry. A Whitmanesque affirmation, this faith is grounded in Nature as life-enhancer and life-giver and revealed in Dickey's treatment of animals as totems and his belief that hunting, once imperative for simple survival, has now become a ritual by which to enter into communion with the animal. Smith declares, however, that while Dickey's faith has its roots in the natural world, it "flowers in myth" (260), a private rather than a traditional mythology where the poet becomes the spiritual guide. Lensing (1978) similarly finds the poetry "an instructive model" (20), but specifically one by which to delineate the origins of an American neo-romanticism. Unlike Gregor (1973), who views Dickey's romanticism as deriving from his essential sense of affirmation, or Kirschten (1988), who argues that it is only one aspect of the poetry where his principle of motion manifests itself, Lensing suggests that the poetic role of personality and the poet's use of "the audacious metaphor" (20) fashion Dickey's voice. The persona enables Dickey's clear identity to undergo a psychic change into another form of life and thereby participate in "a common vitalism" (21). The unity subsequently manifests itself not as a technique but through metaphors which reveal a sense of growing spirituality. Calhoun (1976) discerns a change in Dickey's "poetic constructions of anti-wastelands" (18), though he also observes a continuity in his stress on the survivor. The poet's entrance into middle age simply alters the image of survivor from one of war to his more recent view of escaping from life's destructive forces. Both "Power and Light" and "Falling" show the transistion from *Buckdancer's Choice*, with its emphasis on celebration, to *The Eye-Beaters*, Dickey's "most existential volume" (19), which stresses the necessity of confronting destructive forces and discovering the spiritual means to do so.

Other critics center specifically on particular poems in *Falling*. Pierce (1976), for instance, sees "Adultery" as a poem of survival, not with regard to nature but to the dolorous enervation of daily life, where stale choices and deadened sensibilities bring two people to a room they "cannot die in." The sexually suggestive imagery parallels the movement of the poem to effect "a catharsis and a ritual" (67) that is both "the end of hope and its renewal" (67). Bowers-Hill (1984) considers "The Sheep Child" a poem central in Dickey's poetry to understanding his concept of transcendence, despite Lensing's (1973) view that the poem is "unintentionally comic" (163) and despite Hill's (1973) contention that it reveals Dickey's "discomfort in the presence of the ideal" (149). Bowers-Hill declares that while the animals in "The Heaven of Animals" do not naturally reside in their transcendent condition, having entered it through death, the sheep child is born to it and enjoys a "stasis" (2) that transcends human restrictions and boundaries. It represents "the concrete symbol of the unattainable (in reality) condition man naturally strives for" (6) and allows one to establish "levels of transcendence" (6) among Dickey's poetic creations. Lieberman (1967), however, sees in the poem only the problems of how one who has returned from "nonhuman chosen otherness" (513) connects again with "common chosen humanity" (513), a concern of Dickey's throughout *Falling*. Bobbitt (1978) perceives the creature as another example of "unnatural order" (39). Its existence not only shocks the ordered human world with its avoidance of irrationality but also reveals man's alienation from Nature.

Critics likewise offer diverse perspectives regarding "Falling," the account of a twenty-nine-year-old stewardess accidently swept to her death from the emergency door of an airplane. As with "The Sheep Child," Hill (1973) argues that the poem promises continuity and is therefore comic, unlike tragedy, which suggests rigid containment. While alive, the stewardess "moves in her slim tailored / Uniform," but her fall, during which she removes her clothing in order "to die / Beyond explanation," enables her to become a "life symbol" (146). Her imaginative vision involves a "creative identity with the natural world" (148) and juxtaposes a tragic narrative with a comic belief in "fertile continuance" (148) because the stewardess becomes a fertility goddess "impressed / In the soft loam." While her bird-like flight points toward her "psychic metamorphosis" (Lensing, 1978 21), Peterman (1981) argues that only when the stewardess sheds the clothing that has previously defined her does her exhileration become ecstasy. Feeling her naked body, she turns in the air to meet the earth face up. In so doing, Dickey shows not only the earth seeming to embrace her—"clothing her naturally" (16)—but also intimating her rising from the earth. Her death therefore is both "cataclysmic and rapturous" (17). Lensing (1973) sees in her fall the paradox of a tragic knowledge of imminent death that nevertheless is "a moment of acute consciousness, a coming fully to life" (173), while Tucker (1976) considers that her unusual perspective of the world enables the stewardess to achieve a "more-than-human link with the universe" (5).

Bowers (1985) notes the poem's long split lines and language resembling extemporaneous speech to achieve presentational immediacy. The use of third person distances the speaker, who remains between the reader and the stewardess's experience, but the absence of Dickey's own commentary on the meaning of her impact leaves readers "to find our own applications for the myth, and the process involves us even more deeply in the poem" (49). Calhoun and Hill (1983) see such techniques not as self-promotional but the means to show that the "precipitous mortal plunge" (83) of all human beings can speak of "ecstacy rather than despair" (83). The stewardess becomes symbolic of possibility within the human condition. Given the last words in Dickey's first collected poems, she utters "AH, GOD—," a revelation that releases her in the final mortal experience and which results from Dickey's romantic tendency to originate poems in "surveys of natural surfaces" (Kirschten 54). The stewardess sees "the huge partial form of the world ... lose its evoked master shape," a perspective precipitated by the poetic "mixtures of animated shapes" (94). The setting becomes alive with forces whose mingling produces "a dazzling plentitude of motion" (94). Kirschten also argues that the poem, far from being simply the narrative of a spectacular if accidental fall, ritually reenacts a primitive vegetation rite that assures continuation of the crops and the tribe. In principle and structure, Dickey parallels his modern rite with "an ancient Aztec process of victimage" (119), a ritual involving three parts: the preparation of the victim as a sacrificial surrogate, her execution, and the transference of her extraordinary power to the crops as an act of redemptive regeneration. Yet Baughman (1985) sees the act of the stewardess not as a vicarious sacrifice but as "a symbol of human mortality and human aspiration" (92). Much like Donald Armstrong's final gymnastic feat in "The Performance," she achieves a "last superhuman act" that suggests renewal; but in "Falling" the imagery is sexual and religious.

Because "Falling," the title poem of *Falling* and the final poem in *Poems 1957-1967*, closely resembles in theme and technique "May Day Sermon," which introduces this collection, critics compare them. Bowers (1985), for example, points out the same, long split lines punctuated by gaps in words or phrases. Dickey aims for presentational immediacy by approximating the appearance of a literal printed sermon but one whose irregular blank spacings, which suggest natural pauses in speech, demand it be read aloud, thereby making the reader a participant. Bowers believes that the sermon itself dominates the myth of the young woman. Discovered having had sex with a man her religious father considers objectionable, she first kills him after he ties her to a pole and whips her and then rides off into the woods with her lover. The woman preacher is leaving the Baptist Church and wants to impress her message—the efficacy of the earth's natural rhythms and processes—upon the minds and hearts of other women in the congregation. While in "Falling" the myth of the stewardess turned fertility goddess remains primary, here the sermon which presents the myth captures the reader's attention. Scrutinized together, the two poems represent "variations on a single narrative experiment" (49) where Dickey tests his open form in third- and first-person. Baughman (1985) believes "May Day Sermon" extends "Falling" because the former presents a woman's fall as "a means of salvation" (94) while the latter offers it for womankind. Like "Falling," the protagonist tumbles from an ordered world into one more chaotic and deadly but which offers life-sustaining possibilities. Dickey replaces an airplane with the Baptist Church and the void of cold space and fertile Kansas loam with the fog-shrouded "wilds of passionate sensuality" (94). The "fall from grace" (95) of both the young stewardess and the female minister signals their rise into a more natural grace.

Dickey's increasing use of violence as a thematic concern also evidences itself in the poem, though now presented vicariously through a sermon. Ramsey (1973) calls "May Day Sermon" "the sexual-hysterical rantings of an insane woman preacher" (185), while Kirschten (1988) sees Dickey's depiction of victimage not only "to refresh, transform, and restore nature to an Edenic state" (80), but also to reveal, as the poet writes, "holiness learned in the barn." This violence changes both the poetic agents and the setting "in excessive, orgasmic, even barbaric ways" (83). Like Bowers, Calhoun and Hill (1983) believe that the telling of the story is as important as the actual plot detail because "May Day" depends upon "oratorical excesses" (77). Like Kirschten, moreover, they declare that by violence, either physical, verbal, or imaginative, Dickey enables the lovers, the woman preacher, and the reader "to transcend everyday expectations of the self" (78-79). Clausen (1978) focuses on Dickey's method of using local legend to present the "enunciation of a pantheistic mysticism that glorifies sex" (301). While the sermon is native to the characters, it restricts the poet's voice to that of a preacher whose own voice would be too unsophisticated to embody his attitudes and still remain a valid figure. Dickey circumvents the problem by having the preacher announce his "highly erotic pantheism" (299) through the rhythms and cadences of a Baptist sermon. However, the preacher never explains her motivation and never reveals the psychological depth necessary to justify her dramatic change of belief. Because the poem's central issue is "the whole nature of Puritanism" (301), the woman must possess sufficient "symbolic weight" (301), and she does not. Her behavior and her characterization lack the development to sustain the narrative.

Relatively few critics have presented studies that center exclusively on "May Day." In doing so, Sloan (1969) and Seale (1979) stress the poem's narrative strategy. Sloan argues that "May Day" is a "poem of happening" which exploits the fluidity of speech in order to impose a pattern of experience upon the present moment. Poems of statement, on the contrary, use the permanence of print to lock into time some observation about human experience. Dickey utilizes speech as both the "agent of change" (17) in the preacher's narrative and as the poet's principal "rhetorical strategy" (17). The poem concerns the destruction of barriers, particularly those dictated by unyielding categories of thought, a fact apparent in the poem's long title, because the preacher is leaving one place to join a larger group. Sound effectively removes these barriers by giving "time and space the temporarily and the fluidity of the spoken word" (18). Such language, moreover, yields the sense of the poem's occurring in the present, a kind of violence to the usual view of language as linear and objective. Because violence also pervades the images and actions in the poem, Dickey's "defiant illiteracy" (19) opens the narrative to time and space as the woman preacher similarly asks the women of Gilmer County, Georgia, to open themselves to the spirit that continuously moves through nature and that renews itself each spring.

Seale's examination, less philosophically abstract than Sloan's, emphasizes that the story of the young woman who murders her father to ride away with her one-eyed lover is not the poem; the telling of that narrative is. Unlike Bowers (1985), who suggests that such a deliberate strategy enables Dickey the sell the poem to the reader more easily, Seale states that by deliberately preventing the preacher from achieving a recognizable identity, Dickey allows for her otherwise unjustified poetic eloquence. He eliminates the possibility of imaginative excess by using progressive tenses ("Children, I shall be showing you") and grammatical parallelism ("To the sacks of corn and coal to nails to the swelling ticks"). The absence of sections or divisions contributes to the poem's linguistic momentum, as do the long hexa- and heptametric lines, while sparse punctuation reinforces the oral quality of the poem. Words wholly capitalized show emphasis. Moreover, the blanks within the split line suggest "a kind of heartbeat/drumbeat" (27) that serves as a backdrop against which the story is told, and the long line itself gives the preacher a wide latitude in her sermon, which is often repetitious in both diction and symbol. The sermon's message of "the miracle of life" (30) becomes possible because of "the miracle of how this story is told" (30).

Rose (1978) asserts that the work's power derives from "the technique of 'exchange'" (254), and its message is imparted at the opening of the woman preacher's farewell address: "Each year at this time I shall be telling you of the Lord /... giving men all the help they need / To drag their daughters into barns...." Particularly appropriate is the "curiously powerful ambience" (255) of the South's Bible Belt, whose "aberrant socio-religious beliefs" (256) are contrasted with the ancient fertility rites of May. Rose suggests that the lovers, having returned to nature as archetypes, do not so much escape as become "reborn each year into cyclical infinity" (256). The narrator becomes a yearly example to the Church of its errors, specifically the subjugation of women by encouraging the belief that they lack sexual desire, that they are subordinate to men, and that they caused the Fall. While the preacher escapes male domination, the young woman of whom the preacher speaks does not. Playing the role of Odysseus, she will constantly have to elude men who, like the Cyclops, will seek to eat her alive in "a pattern of events which extend into perpetuity" (256). The poem's mystical quality lies both in the transformation of the preacher by the barn experience she relates, a symbol of "the savage source of the vital, the primal, within us all" (257), and in her transfiguration of the congregation through an exchange with "the girl who is now inside us" (257). Dickey, in effect, inverts the Eden myth and reveals an empathy toward women oppressed by men. Rather than having the girl die as punishment for her sin, she is reborn each May to reaffirm her needs and possibilities.

Pair's critical examination, "'Dancing With God': Totemism in Dickey's 'May Day Sermon'," appears in the volume on Dickey by G.K. Hall for its *Critical Essays* series. Pair provides an anthropological and ethnological interpretation. To dramatize the cruelty of those who use religion villainously, Dickey "re-visions" a legend about a house avoided by local people because of the patricide that occurred there and their belief that the woman and her lover, killed when their motorcycle plunges off the road, return each spring. Dickey himself asserts in *Self-Interviews* that the poem concerns "the absorption of these details into the minds of the community" (183), a process that has "something to do with the engrained attitude of mythologizing that rural communities have. What originated as a story of rural blood lust and religion and sex and escape has now become something of a legend" (183-84). Pair argues that the connection between the Baptist Church, with its belief in original sin, and the legend, with its elements of blood lust, religion, sex, and escape, constitutes a cultural bond involving modern religion and primitive animism. This relationship involves Dickey's process of exchange. The poem, moreover, creates "a meta-mythology," an examination of the study of myth. Dickey exchanges the pagan divinity with the newer Christian mythology to create "a protoculture," a connection established through the use of totem. In establishing "a myth of two totemic clans," the poet juxtaposes two religions. A four-part totem, consisting of fog, gamecock, snake, and neighbor/lover, represents the patriarchal Christian religion, and the tree, considered divine by primitive religions, becomes the opposing animistic totem. By contrasting these "clan symbols," while simultaneously revealing their common origin, "May Day Sermon" transcends its rural setting to establish a mythology in which "primitive and modern humankind demonstrate the timeless unity of blood acts, the mind, and the spiritual consciousness." Aware of both views, the preacher presents mystic totems that simultaneously represent the Christian patriarchy of the father and the young male lover and an implied totemic May Pole that suggests the primitive matriarchal society of both the speaker and the female hero. The sermon clearly shows that the religion of the modern Baptist community dominates as ineffectually as ancient rites and that women justifiably seek their sexual freedom as they search for regenerative possibilities.

3: Initiation: *The Eye-Beaters, Blood, Victory, Madness, Buckhead and Mercy*

BUCKDANCER'S CHOICE AND FALLING culminate Dickey's entrance into poetry undertaken with *Into the Stone* and continued with *Drowning With Others* and *Helmets*. They also exhibit poetic techniques that suggest a distinctly different, verbal experimentalism. The early motion reveals an interest not only in anecdotal narratives but also in ideal forms and an exchange with some other being. Initially presented in an incantatory, essentially anapestic meter featuring italicized refrains, it yields to the beginnings of a movement where long lines, gapped with words and phrases, physically confront the reader to provide presentational immediacy. While this central motion opens itself, as it were, to invite a shared participation, it offers no real sense of closure, of ideas and attitudes being definitively decided. Dickey's principal thematic concerns of family, war, death, and love remain, but they broaden to reveal a social consciousness. The publication in 1970 of *The Eye-Beaters, Blood, Victory, Madness, Buckhead and Mercy* fully displays Dickey's heightened poetic ability and realizes his central motion. Not only does the title poem extend the block format, but the volume also exhibits in another of its poems, "Pine," the beginning of a future poetic direction, where the poem appears precariously balanced or suspended on the printed page. Moreover, Dickey's sense of affirmation, his innate belief in imaginative possibilities, becomes more tenuous and strained than in previous volumes. These considerations suggest that *The Eye-Beaters* marks the full initiation into the poetic journey that Dickey began a decade earlier.

Despite its important position in Dickey's canon, *The Eye-Beaters, Blood, Victory, Madness, Buckhead and Mercy* has received scant critical attention. Early commentary was unfavorable, largely because reviewers perceived the poetic technique as prosaic. Shaw (1971) believes the volume full of "long-winded, loquacious poems, springing from a milieu of tale tales, yarns, leisurely long-summer-evening-front-porch stories" (230). In effect, the poet insistently talks *to* the reader rather than engaging him imaginatively. The gap-stopped lines build tension in a poem like "Madness," but in "The Eye-Beaters," this spacing technique seems only "chronic stutter" (230). Shaw singles out "Pine" for its "florid, Hopkins-like language" (230), which contrasts markedly with the otherwise clotted, feeble, or bathetic quality of the poems. Fraser (1971-1972) faults the poems for containing irrelevant detail. While interesting biographically or topographically, the extraneous material suggests that Dickey's poetic technique involves incorporating everything into the poem in the hope that, unplanned, it will somehow naturally cohere into a whole.

Yet some critics initially recognized the distinctiveness of *The Eye-Beaters* even as they faulted it. Liebowitz (1970) asserts that Dickey has long attempted to reconcile nature with "the household gods of order" (20) and, through "the miracles of motion" and "an ecstasy of pure art" (20), to discover his fundamental position regarding them. His previous poetry reveals a private understanding that was "magic without primitivism, spiritual grace without mysticism" (20). However, in *The Eye-Beaters* this understanding fragments, the splintering indicated by the overblown title. As Dickey's material is stretched ever more thinly, his voice becomes "public, forensic, even maudlin" (22). Citing "Looking for the Buckhead Boys," "Living There," and "Mercy" as examples, Liebowitz says Dickey flounders in a "poetic backwater" (22), and a hysteria that closely resembles "childish petulance" (22) pervades the poems. They offer few new answers to what the critic sees as "self-mistrust and backsliding" (22). Even the title poem constitutes a debate about the future course of Dickey's art. DeMott (1970) also discerns a difference in the volume, calling it "death-obsessed, dense with assault and pain" (26), and declaring that while Dickey continues to draw on "more-life materials and assumptions" (26), the explicitness is new. He still physically endeavors to grasp and master the world's energy and violence, utilizing all imaginative resources in the effort. However, the danger resides in the poems seeming "a contrivance for one particular aptitude" (26) that lacks form and becomes directionless. Because Dickey achieves "high excitement—or explosion" (38), DeMott concludes that the poet sacrifices everything on "the altar of projective power" (38).

Critics such as Howard (1966) and Davison (1967) earlier recognized the qualities of obsession and violence in *Buckdancer's Choice*, but where previous scholarship only saw Dickey turning outward amid this disorder, assessment now also discerns the evolution of a new self. As this persona struggles to emerge, his voice appropriately becomes more colloquial. Oates (1974) considers some of the poems "bluntly confessional" (131) because the poet engages in "a battle with his soul" (132) by raising so many unanswered questions. Haule (1979) observes speech distinctive of the rural South and suggests that because Dickey no longer struggles "to find an end" (44), he assumes a conversational syntax. Compressed, memorable images yield to an expansiveness as the poet's language now unites with his poetic form to avoid pretense. Calhoun and Hill (1983), noting that *The Eye-Beaters* "severely demarcates" the later poetry, similarly discern "a new oratorical tone" (85) as the poems show decidedly human efforts through "an extraordinary metaphysics of excess" (85).

Bly's criticism of Dickey for failing vocally to condemn the Vietnam war did not stop Dickey during this time from reading public poems, such as "Exchanges," the Phi Beta Kappa poem presented at Harvard in 1970, and "The Strength of Fields," Jimmy Carter's inaugural poem given in 1977. In *The Eye-Beaters*, public and private poems dominate, but others like "Pine,"

"Turning Away," and "Madness" anticipate the poet's later, almost imagistic poetry. The volume contains Dickey's "first studiedly public poems between book covers" (Calhoun and Hill 86)—"In the Pocket," written for *Life* on behalf of the National Football League, and again for *Life*, "Apollo," which celebrates the manned moon missions. In these, Dickey is more assertive and insistent because of "the necessity of transcendence" (88). Other poems are personal not so much because of their autobiographical nature or subject matter as because of "a very particular narrative voice" (89). Like Haule, Calhoun and Hill discern an informality that is "engaging but forceful" (89). An educated man expressing common passions, Dickey gives a performance resembling "a good storyteller with his friends" (89). While not confessional in the usual introspective manner, the poems are "public-personal" (89), requiring an audience not to overhear but to participate. While the early motion is structured dramatically, with only a few poems depending for their organization upon the narrator's directly addressing another figure, most of the poems in *The Eye-Beaters* speak either to some aspect of the narrator's own Self, as in "Sugar" and "Under Buzzards," or to the poet's family, as in "Butterflies" and "Giving a Son to the Sea." Other poems like "Mercy" do have the speaker meeting someone accompanied by a vaguely defined companion that Dickey calls "we." "Diabetes" has the narrator alternatingly address himself, his audience, and his characters. When taken collectively, "Living Together" and "Looking for the Buckhead Boys," the two poems comprising "Two Poems of Going Home," move from a narrative voice "introspective, metaphysical, and relatively tense" (93) to one more social. These public-personal poems attempt to discover "regeneration in the passionate speech of the common man" (94) by stretching language to embrace the widest range of emotions, trying to elevate readers from the ordinary and enervating toward more intense experiences.

Baughman's (1978) thorough analysis of *The Eye-Beaters* asserts that a new self emerges which culminates Dickey's long search of "transformation, exploration, and ... 'exchanges of identity'" (81). This self results from his awareness of an endless, devastating flux that, instead of being a medium of connection with some other person, is now the object of the poet's scrutiny. Against an external chaos characterized by loss and failed transcendence, the self seeks "a core of emotional stability" (81) that increasingly becomes undercut by the results of change—age, disease, doubt, and fear. While it fails to triumph against the forces opposing it, it nevertheless achieves a kind of glory in the momentary victory of the struggle itself. "Knock," "Diabetes," and "The Cancer Match" introduce Dickey's old self and function as a transition to the new, providing the speaker with external and internal threats that physically and spiritually undermine his world. When the narrator in "The Cancer Match" declares, "Internally, I rise like my old self / To watch ... O Self, like a beloved son," the new self emerges, determined not to yield to doubt but clearly conscious of its isolation. What then follows is the poet's re-examination of his old themes: war ("Victory"), family ("Messages"), society ("Two Poems of Going Home"), love ("Mercy" and

"Blood"), the self's relation to society ("The Eye-Beaters"), and nature ("Pine"). Struggling for order, Dickey learns that he has survived war only to win a troubled peace; that he loves his children only to discover they must eventually leave home; that he can return to the place of his youth but find only loss and dislocation; and that while he can enter nature and achieve union with its forms, such communion quickly ends. When he finally looks at his life and merely sees alienation, he realizes that his experiences have all been "Variations on Estrangement," the subtitle of "Living There," but that he must continue the search. The self now recognizes that it can learn the answers about life but that they likely will come, as Dickey writes at the conclusion of this poem, "Later, much later, on."

Calhoun (1971) similarly observes the concerns with aging, mortality, and the sense of loss and despair that characterize the poems. They deal essentially with "situations from which there is no escape" (12), and he labels *The Eye-Beaters* Dickey's "most existential volume" (12). Problems of rhetoric consequently evidence themselves, including a profusion of interjections and apostrophes and the use of rhetorical questions. Occasionally, Dickey's style seems developing in opposite directions. While in a poem like "The Eye-Beaters" he transcends his earlier "big forms" (12) toward archetypal imagery, he also echoes early poems by using simple, direct statements and concluding only with the mundane or trite. When discussing illnesses in "Under Buzzards," he even resembles Robert Lowell rather than projecting the expansiveness of his early motion. Despite such problems, *The Eye-Beaters* argues that in confronting real or imagined situations, often involving the fear of death, the individual must deliberately risk himself to expose the value of life.

McNamara (1986) specifically examines the title poem, which concerns the efforts of a narrator to understand why the children in an institution for the blind strike their eyes. His discourse becomes a debate between his reason and "his invention" when he learns that they try to see sparks of light with their physical violence. Viewing the poem as an attempt to determine whether art can understand "the mystery of human suffering" (20), McNamara discerns a two-track narrative strategy: the poem itself records in a block format the interior debate while the marginal prose gloss provides "a spatial and temporal record" (20) of the confrontation. These interact to provide "the progress of a man's inner and outer vision" (20). Moreover, while the explanatory gloss is dry and matter-of-fact, relating only exterior actions, the poem by contrast presents long, enjambed lines punctuated with caesuras and blank spaces. These contribute to "a prayer-like, incantatory rhythm" (21), as when the narrator emphatically asserts: "Come something come blood sunlight come and they break...." The strategy parallels Dickey's conception of a dualistic world and affirms, against a self-defeating nihilism, the power of the imagination to understand suffering.

In the spring 1992 issue of the *James Dickey Newsletter*, Mapp acknowledges the presence of an inner and outer vision but argues that "The Eye-Beaters" is integrated with the volume's other poems through a pattern of images involving children, blindness, and hunting. As such, it culminates the book by revealing most fully "the powerlessness of humanity to save itself physically" (27). Although Dickey effectively sections the poem through his prose gloss, "The Eye-Beaters" exhibits a psychological division regarding the speaker's growth. Four stages progressively move from the concrete to the abstract and from the real to the fictional as the unnamed narrator proceeds from non-involvement to full participation in the children's tragedy, steps that reflect the conditions of reality, fiction, conflict, and the acceptance of fiction. In the inital stage, realism dominates as the persona confronts the tragedy of frightened children who suffer physical defects they cannot comprehend. The children, rather than the speaker, are the central focus; lacking vision, they have fundamentally lost their freedom. As in "Diabetes," where the narrator hopelessly endures a life of "needles moderation / And exercise," the children are figuratively dead. Their violent physical actions resemble madness, and their irrational utterances suggest primitive, instinctual man. Efforts to "see" only bring more pain, a situation analogous to that in "Madness," where a dog reacting to its sexual instincts acquires rabies and must be trapped and killed. Watching the children strike themselves, the stranger discards this painful reality for a fiction that will impart meaning to the experience. While the children remain the central figures in the poem's second stage, the focus becomes the fiction he creates to save his sanity by paradoxically involving himself in the children's lives. As in "Messages" and "Two Poems of Going Home," the narrator cannot save the children. However, Dickey juxtaposes blindness with internal vision to suggest that the former promotes the latter and "thus creates as well as destroys" (29). Moreover, both the children and narrator resemble God because, as the children imaginatively create primordial images that involve animals, cave art, and hunting, their actions cause the speaker in turn to imagine their creating them. As he becomes more involved in these racial memories, reality intrudes, and "his internal vision is temporarily suspended by his outer vision" (31). He recognizes that he cannot save the children and that his fiction is for himself, a situation similar to that in "Mercy," where a nurse realizes she fails to help her patients. "The Eye-Beaters" remains tragic until the very end when the speaker accepts the fiction that he can impart to the children their vision: "I am trying to make it   make something   make them / make me / Re-invent the vision of the race   knowing the blind must see / By magic or nothing." Inner vision becomes, Mapp declares, "the only tool for survival" (33). Just as the children continue by means of their eye-beating and their "magical art," so does the race through instinct and imagination. By becoming "imaginative, instinctual Man" (34), the narrator shows that deliverance exists within the individual's own mind.

While "The Eye-Beaters" resembles earlier poems like "Falling," "Slave Quarters," and "May Day Sermon" in block format, Raymond Smith (1972) labels the new poem a "mythic vision" (269) and, more than McNamara, suggests its universality by declaring that the narrator's predicament is that of modern man. Rationalism, connoted by the image of the sun, has blinded him to the efficacy of his own racial myths; to survive he needs "new art" (271). Rather than accept a philosophy of art for art's sake, the poet returns to the collective unconscious to seek "the healing, life-sustaining roots of his past" (272). He deliberately chooses the richness of illusion, and art becomes a desperate and bloody affair; or as Dickey writes, "I pass beyond in secret in perversity and the sheer / Despair of invention." Consequently, "The Eye-Beaters" affirms Dickey's categorical belief in "the mythmaking power of man" (272), a faith in art's redemptive power that unifies all his poetry despite a growing sense of mortality. That faith is similar to Dickey's use of romantic principles to depict how poetry yields "emotional compensation for dramatic problems" (Kirschten 90). While the poet realizes his attempts to create "a poetic function of primitive magical therapy" (90) will fail, the self achieves a momentary knowledge that poetic utterance precludes "spiritual death" (Baughman 85). That the blind children also try "for light and life through art" (85) underscores Dickey's focus on the individual.

Oates, however, argues that the poem's passionate tone, its "dramatic ferocity" (138), suggests the abandonment of faith in one religion (art) and a tentative acceptance of another (the "Beast"). Dickey's presence in *The Eye-Beaters* is conspicuous, admitting everything as he wars against himself and seeks a deliverance. Unable to compromise with a world that cannot understand him, he courts the primitive because "the release offerred by words no longer satisfies" (138-39). Ritual has become so obviously a contrived game that his consciousness splits into different levels of awareness. The self becomes estranged and, aware that mortality and disease corrupt physical prowess, projects its suffering outward with a demand so vast, it excludes the personal for the universe itself. Yet the desire is itself "a kind of miracle or reincarnation" (141). "Turning Away," the concluding poem, shows the need to transcend the physical by embracing the timeless, and Oates asserts that having explored variations of unity and dissolution, Dickey now seems poised in a new direction.

Calhoun and Hill (1983) call "The Eye-Beaters" the most important poem in the volume, declaring its technique "experimental; its process, archetypal; and its blunt optimism at the end, almost Victorian" (96). However, another poem, "Pine," foreshadows Dickey's later, almost imagistic works, including *Puella* (1982). In the preface to *The Central Motion* (1983), Dickey comments on the evolution of his poetic technique: "After 'Falling,' 'The Fiend,' and 'May Day Sermon,' I wrote only one more poem in what I call 'block format'; this was 'The Eye-Beaters,' and it may be the best of them. The book in which it appears also marked the beginning of the verbal experimentalism—in 'Pine,' particularly—that led to the poems of *Puella* and the poems after it" (v). Baughman (1985) sees "Pine" as reflecting "the stance of the artist" (103). Using "associational imagery" (*Sorties* 96), the poem presents the speaker's progressive efforts to unite himself with nature by identifying with the tree's physical and intuited qualities. Subtitled "successive apprehensions," it moves through five parts, from a "primitive, sensual response" (104) for the wind held by the tree, then to the speaker's tasting a piece of pine, until finally he climbs its rough exterior to the top where he embraces "it all / Together" to discover "Glory." Art and nature momentarily combine to bring "wholeness" (Baughman 105). The poem aspires to a sensuous, nonrational understanding of the natural realm, a goal which accounts for the poetic language that masks the narrator almost completely. Dickey restructures sense impressions synaesthetically by freeing the imagination among the tree's qualities for the speaker to assimilate or gather (Calhoun and Hill 94). Kirschten (1988) sees these efforts to accumulate "a complex perception" (178) as a magical means for the narrator to arrive at "his gerundive world of constant motion" (178). In this progress, art becomes "the medium of exchange for synesthetic perception" (56).

4: *The Zodiac* and *The Strength of Fields*

TOTALING SIXTY-TWO PAGES WHEN originally published and divided into twelve sections, *The Zodiac* (1976) became Dickey's single most ambitious effort. In its sprawling format and split-line technique, the poem resembles such previous efforts as "Falling" and "May Day Sermon." Yet Dickey's use of a translated text which he then re-invents, his gradual merging of perspectives, and his transformation of a traditional Christian myth into a personal and universal mythology that comments on the nature of art and the artist—these render *The Zodiac* altogether unique. Discussing the poem in the preface to *The Central Motion*, Dickey declares:

> I sought to deal with risks, and take them, and to have my spokesman exemplify the conviction that the poet must go all-out for his vision, his angle, as it presents itself *at that moment*. A good deal of *The Zodiac* is the self-hypnotized yammering and assertiveness of a drunk, but a drunk who would not be able to achieve his occasionally clear and perhaps deep focus on matters of concern to him unless he had had his inhibitions broken down—or through—by the dangerous means he employs, for he insists on nothing less than a personal connection between an exalted and/or intoxicated state, the starry universe, the condition he calls Time, and words. Taking off from Hendrik Marsman's respectable and ambitious poem and re-inventing almost everything in it, I tried to present a number of states of mind in which the cosmos changes, moment to moment in a single consciousness, from a display of miracles to a delusional nightmare—the horrors of delirium tremens—and then back, all changes being parts of its encounter with that hugely mortal beast, the universe, and the smaller, mega-billion-miled Forms, the animals that comprise some of it, in their stark, hinting, and timorous patterns. (v-vi)

Marsman's poem, "De Dierenriem" (1940), translated from the Dutch by A.J. Barnouw, was re-titled *The Zodiac* in the spring 1947 issue of the *Sewanee Review* while Dickey was attending Vanderbilt. Reprinted the following year in Barnouw's anthology *Coming After: An Anthology from the Low Countries* (1948), the translation served as the narrative basis for Dickey's longer effort.

Critics generally consider *The Zodiac* a flawed masterpiece. In its stylistic ambitiousness, Warren (1976) compares the poem to Hart Crane's "The Bridge." Despite a vaguely defined structural principle in the opening half of the work and "some sort of structural blockage" (8) in the concluding two parts, the bold imagery as well as the varied rhythms "redeems all" (8). The narrative concerns the efforts of a drunken Dutch poet to relate himself through words to the stars, believing that poetry is "the enunciation of universality" (8), though *The Zodiac* more pointedly details "the over-ambitiousness of poetry—even as it celebrates its ambitiousness" (8). Prescott (1976) compares the poem to Berryman's "Homage to Mistress Bradstreet." Dickey's long lines, consisting of word clusters, are at times "wonderfully charged" and at other times "loose to the point of prosiness" (89), as when Dickey writes, "Ah, to hell with it: he can't quit. / Neither can you, reader." Prescott, however, declares that the poem reveals a "progression toward eloquence" (89) that concludes with the human endeavor to find meaning: "Make what it can of what is: / So long as the spirit hurls on space / The star-beasts of intellect and madness." Its focus is "man's purpose, his despair and his eventual triumph" (89).

While noting the poem's "raw vitalism" and "convincing speech" (1), Burnshaw (1976) confronts the issue of Dickey's use of Marsman's poem, a concern addressed by other critics as well. Dickey himself writes in the headnote to the volume:

> This poem is based on another of the same title. It was written by Hendrik Marsman, who was killed by a torpedo in the North Atlantic in 1940. It is in no sense a translation, for the liberties I have taken with Marsman's original poem are such that the poem I publish here, with the exception of a few lines, is completely my own.

Burnshaw states that although the story-line of the two works is "fairly close" (1), Dickey's poem is considerably longer and offers his new conception of the hero: "A drunken and perhaps dying Dutch poet who returns to his home in Amsterdam after years of travel and tries desperately to relate himself, by means of stars, to the universe." Marsman's narrator, moreover, describes and interprets the hero in conventional verse patterns, while the hero himself speaks in Dickey's work, often cursing God or streaming with a vision. His words are like "a prosody music-score" (1) with the margins and spacings reflecting the haphazard processes of a larger-than-life man struggling through whiskey to hold the stars. Because the poem affirms the ability of the imagination to conceive the world by overcoming its distinctions, poetry becomes, by extension, "an instrument for human survival" (1).

However, Dickey's indebtedness to Marsman's poem troubles Cassity (1981), who believes his version too much resembles the original. Evaluating *The Zodiac* section by section and periodically comparing it to Marsman's, Cassity believes the former adheres too closely for no discernible reason, calling Dickey's version a "compromise" of what he obviously intends as "his artistic testament with the hint of plagiarism" (192). In one of the few critical essays dedicated exclusively to *The Zodiac*, Heylen (1990) broadens this issue and addresses the larger problems involved with a process Dickey believes to be not translation but the creation of a new poem. She argues that the poem is about "interpreting and writing, and thus also about translating" (2). It is, moreover, "a self-translation by and of a poet who cannot escape his self and who delivers a pastiche of his own poetics" (2) where he reveals not a prescription for writing poetry but a performance of it. Given a narrative framework with certain images and motifs, he uses lyricism to exhibit through deliberate "stage-managing" (3) how to read and then re-write a translation. Comparison of Dickey's poem and Barnouw's translation underscores their differences. Dickey's tone is aggressive; his voice, Dionysian; the imagery, less Biblical and more alive. Unlike most translations, moreover, Dickey's work does not display qualities or characteristics different from his own poetry; rather, his style and language remain observable. His version is "more subjective than imitation and more visceral than paraphrase" (3). Dickey's creative process emphasizes the poetic task by showing that, after subject and form become determined, poetry's literal state remains lacking without "the theme of imagination and creativity" (4). Beginning in the fourth section of *The Zodiac*, he introduces much less new material either because he became less energetic about the project or because the experiences depicted became too far removed from his own interests. The governing philosophy throughout, however, is one of faith to Marsman and not fidelity to Barnouw, a supposition justified by the way Dickey's own poetic voice pervades *The Zodiac* and the way he re-invents the protagonist to the extent that in the first three sections the narrator and the drunken Dutch poet merge. In approaching Barnouw's translation, therefore, Dickey decided "to write *his* Zodiac because he identified personally with its protagonist" (11). In doing so, he exposed his own techniques and consciousness.

Unlike Warren (1976) and Prescott (1976) who seek to characterize the poem by juxtaposing it with other epic-like modern works, Lensing (1978) places *The Zodiac* in the context of Dickey's romantic tendencies. The poem marks a change in his understanding and places him in the tradition of Whitman and Crane rather than Wright or Stafford. His romantic ideal becomes not the "fusion of inner and outer states" (*Babel to Byzantium* 287), as with the early motion, but the vision captured verbally that not only defines the limits of poetic ambition but which signals the failure of such an endeavor in its inherent elusiveness. Despite critical opinion to the contrary, *The Zodiac* concerns not so much the failed poetic search as "the various departures in quest of it" (28). Two qualities differentiate it from Dickey's usual method: first, the personalities of the speaker and the persona are separate, though the division diminishes as the poem advances until the narrator occasionally merges with the persona's consciousness, and second, the persona's self is never psychically re-oriented by merging with other forms of life. However, Lensing faults the poem not only for "the subjective intensity" (28) of the speaker, where Dickey uses an alcoholic stupor to justify the "near-manic urgency" (28) of his observations and visions, but also for lapses in the personal monologue, where to sustain effect he relies on word repetition, exclamation marks, and capitalization. The drunken poet searches for a more permanent vision than previous personae, one that will conquer "the hammer-clawed stars of death," but transcendent affirmation no longer seems possible because Dickey's faith in imaginative possibilities becomes "more qualified" (31), a view that suggests "the anti-romantic" (31). The poem's triumph resides only in the effort.

Other reviewers and critics believe *The Zodiac* more seriously flawed. Lask (1977) declares that the poem simply fails to persuade and faults not only "its clotted lines and convoluted ideas" (19) but also Dickey's "too strident language," which includes "too many emphases, too many capitalized words, too many italics" (19). The verse seems "roughed up" (19), as if he strains to make it "virile" (19). Kirschten (1988) considers the poem's structure vague. The stages that reveal the Dutch poet's progress remain indeterminate, and *The Zodiac* consequently does not cohere. While the structure need not be temporal but perhaps suggested through rituals that provide guidance and value to the actions of the protagonist, the absence of narrative progression of any sort and the presence only of "page after page of cosmic metaphor" (212) quickly cause the poem to lose both its focus and reader interest.

Mizejewski (1978) contends that the poem exhibits all the themes of Dickey's early work, including his beliefs that the poet is part of history, that man is estranged from nature and able only momentarily to enter it through an imaginative transcendence, and that language becomes a ritual magic against mortality (412). Yet *The Zodiac* also reveals "an actor-poet who has gone as far as he can, almost on a dare, into a painful, public exploration of trauma" (411). Rather than adopt a confessional personality like that of Lowell, Berryman, or Sexton, Dickey selects that of "shaman, wizard, showman" (411). Because the poem awed as well as confused reviewers, Mizejewski explores the reasons for its perceived critical failure. Among them are Dickey's inability to develop a character magnificently brilliant in his drunkenness, the failure to link his protagonist's fall with the decline of western civilization and the rise of Fascism and Nazism, the use of forced or bombastic metaphors to appropriate the external world into the Zodiac poet's psyche, problems in tone caused by ambiguous shifts from objective narrator to interior monologue, diction and sociology inappropriate to the speaker, and the failure of the poem's form to resolve the problems of the drunken poet such that the structure remains only "a looser pattern of drunkenness, ambition, self-reproach, and finally hope" (417). Moreover, though Dickey attempts to avoid the problems of confessionalism by selecting a character historically and geographically removed from himself, the poem nevertheless manifests the dangers of such poetry: justifying concern in the detailed psychology of the speaker, asking metaphor to humanize an alien world, and requiring the imagination to transcend intense subjectivity to effect an artistic resolution (418).

Dave Smith (1981) faults the poem's lack of narrative and, by entension, the events which would cause the emotional excess. Like Warren (1976) and Kirschten (1988), he also discerns an organizational problem, claiming that the twelve zodiacal sections do nothing to display "the Pythagorean aura of divine immanence" (352). Ideas of time and space are sketched largely but never dramatically justified or progressively developed. Yet Smith sees *The Zodiac* as a transitional poem and labels it "an impressive failure" (352). Dickey has always moved between the social world and the realm of nature, but behind such imaginative journeying lies the fear that man remains "the powerless stranger, a spectre of himself" (349) who desperately seeks an energized union. Since *Poems 1957-1967*, he has relied less on narrative or linear progression and more on a "spacial experience, which in spite of talky rhetoric consists of image and verbal density" (351). *The Zodiac* reflects a poetic progression which in form has been "Faustian: from lyric to epic" (351) and which in theme has shown modern man's increasing estrangement from the universe in the hope that poetry can redeem all. Because everything to which the drunken Dutch poet turns becomes a betrayal, the poem is "entirely self-referential" (352), leaving him aware of his isolation and the emptiness of illusion.

Skipp (1981) calls *The Zodiac* "a major work" (1) and argues that the drunken poet's obsessions render him "a redeemer of time-bound man" (4). By replacing the zodiacal constellation Cancer, Dickey's metonymy for time (4), with his own creation, a Lobster, the speaker reveals humanity's awareness of its own mortality. Therefore, his art becomes sacrificial: "The instrument   the tuning-fork— / He'll flick it with his bandless wedding-finger— / ... So long as the hand can hold its island / Of blazing paper, and bleed for its images." While the Dutch poet fails to find the form necessary to express his simultaneous understanding also of man's divinity, Dickey does, having told the story reflexively through a narrator whose voice assumes an "outer reality" (9).

Van Ness (1985) examines the organizational structure of *The Zodiac*, one of the poem's most cited faults. He states that critics like Dave Smith (1981) and Skipp (1981) misread the work when they declare that it occurs over one day or that its division into twelve sections relates to the zodiac. Calhoun and Hill (1983) also misinterpret the poem when they assert that it follows the classical unities of time, place, and action. The Dutch poet receives his piercing vision, but he ironically fails to pen it because truth resides in flux. Any fusion of inner and outer states, any "linked metaphysics" (2), is transitory. Therefore, the poetic imagination can discern not only a vital world but one that constantly renews itself. Because the protagonist must share that understanding for the poetic role to be meaningful, Van Ness similarly sees the drunken poet as a redeemer, but he argues that the poet is also a fallen man isolated from the physical and social worlds and divided within himself, too self-involved to achieve the aesthetic distance necessary to write the ultimate poem. Appropriately, the drunken poet undergoes a resurrection that occurs over a three-day period, his resurrection and redemption coming on the final day. Such allusions to Christ constitute an essential part of the poem's structure; they recur each day, occasionally being deflated so that the protagonist will remain "recognizably human and not excessively ethereal" (3), but nevertheless becoming more convincing as the poet himself develops. Gradually, he understands not the abstractions of time, space, love, and sex, but their realities. Moreover, *The Zodiac* is as much Dickey's own effort to achieve sublimity as of the drunken poet to relate himself to "God's scrambled zoo" because he alternates his own narrative voice with that of his persona until they merge. The vision of the Dutchman is therefore reflexively presented but at the poem's conclusion expands to the universal, the goal of all poetry.

Baughman's (1985) study ignores the controversy regarding the question of originality and declares that Dickey has increasingly experimented as his career developed. Admitting that the twelve-part framework has no correspondence with the zodiac, Baughman declares instead that the organization is tied to the protagonist's experiences and perceptions. Part 1, comprising almost half the poem, establishes the character of the Dutch poet, his situation, and his struggling efforts to comprehend time, history, and the cosmos. Parts 2 through 7 present his exploration of human understanding and its limitations, including the fields of mathematics and philosophy. Through dreams, memory, and fantasy, he scrutinizes his own life, abandoning reason in parts 8 through 11 and adopting "the more expansive imagination" (124). Finally, in the concluding section, the Dutch poet achieves a serenity with himself and the universe, knowing he will determine his own life and art. While *The Zodiac* clearly dramatizes Dickey's belief in the redemptive power of the imagination, Baughman asserts that it only partly succeeds because of the confusion regarding point of view. The voice of a European speaker periodically becomes indistinguishable from that of a second speaker, what Baughman calls "an omniscient 'I'" (123).

Calhoun and Hill (1983) believe the uncertain critical reception and the lack of any subsequent reputation leave the poem "ungrounded and untended ... waiting for oblivion or some hearty defense" (98). The book's printed format, suggesting in its short, wide pages a quickly-read children's work, and its use of a Dutch narrator whose speech patterns clearly reveal him an American, mitigate serious critical attention. Nevertheless, unlike Smith (1981), Calhoun and Hill view the poem not as a transition but a culmination both of Dickey's "theme of transcendence" (99) and his development of "a very American postmodern narrator" (99). The drunken poet is not broken at the conclusion but "wisely resolved that his art-effort, the poetry of his life, may have consequence" (101). Baughman also considers the poem a culmination because in it Dickey breaks "the confines of a former Self" (129), revitalizing his art such that the volume's affirmative tone anticipates *The Strength of Fields* (1979) and the Dutchman's "intellect and madness" influence the lyricism of *Puella* (1982).

Morris (1982) details earlier themes that influence *The Zodiac*. His intent is to depict Dickey's broad interest not only in the relationship between the

Self and the world but also the effort to enhance, destroy, or restore that connection. For Dickey, the unity resides in images celebrating the instinctive, amoral qualities of animals that men share but which remain hidden or forgotten ("The Sheep Child" and "The Heaven of Animals"). Often his speakers, having lost the "varieties of bestiality" (32), unsuccessfully try to achieve this savage state of being. Such efforts denote a fundamental disharmony between man and nature and the poetic need to find and concisely present some ideal form that reveals "the full power of the id-like, primal force" (33) ("The Movement of Fish"). Dickey's personae discover, however, that while "such moments doubtlessly exist, they are ontologically inaccessible" (34) because the presence of the human observer alters the situation. Such a feature explains Dickey's distinctive voice, "the tone of awe and terror which seems to emanate from beyond any particular, discrete, point of view" (34). This voice also reflects Dickey's "megalomanical ambition" (34) to attain a God-like perspective that dissolves all differences and which encompasses the human cycle of birth, growth, and death while simultaneously seeming outside it ("Encounter in the Cage Country").

Because a transcendent exchange is impossible in life, each Dickey poem fails to present a sustaining image even as it attempts "a new assault on the insoluable" (35). The best examples of this transcendent image often occur when the persona directly confronts death ("Sled Burial, Dream Ceremony," "Looking for the Buckhead Boys," "The Firebombing," and "For the Nightly Ascent of the Hunter Orion over a Forest Clearing"). Morris sees as Dickey's poetic quest the creation of a new vision from the demise of the old, "the poet's sole but mandatory obligation" (36). This likewise constitutes the search of the drunken Dutch poet in *The Zodiac*. Yet Dickey's allusion to older, obscure poets such as Stickney ("Exchanges") and Marsman highlights the futility of this effort. The poet's final disillusion would be to abandon the very effort at secular transcendence which has previously motivated him, a despair that pervades *The Zodiac* (38). Re-creating the zodiac to include a Lobster instead of a Crab reflects Dickey's lifelong struggle to establish continuity with nature and between man and his "bestial" instincts (38). However, while the persona's voice strives to supercede God's through images that are more valid, the attempt to discover "the impossible image" (40) through an imperative of continual transformation also constitutes Dickey's own struggles to transcend his earlier work and, by extension, his own self.

Divided into two separate sections, *The Strength of Fields* epitomizes the diversity of critical opinion that surrounds Dickey's poetry and, in particular, the relatively scant attention it has received since publication of *The Eye-Beaters* (1970). Uncertain how to respond to the new motion, critics have reserved judgment of his experiments in technique. Calhoun and Hill (1983), for example, merely conclude that the book is "mostly just a collection—a good one, but not particularly fresh" (102), calling it "a gathering of forces" (102) or culmination of the literary methods Dickey has previously used. Ten of the poems in "The Strength of Fields" portion were published prior to

1973 and consequently reflect the style of the later works in *Poems 1957-1967* and the poems in *The Eye-Beaters*. The poems in the opening section are not walls of words; but as Dave Smith (1981) has observed, they lack such standard poetic conventions as continuous left-hand margins, the use of stanzas and a repetitive line-length, and consistent punctuation (353). Dickey's avoidance of such practices emphasizes that he is still working less with narrative than with "spatial suspension of states of being" (353). *The Strength of Fields* also contains a section entitled "Head-Deep in Strange Sounds: Free-Flight Improvisations from the unEnglish," a group of fourteen poems that are not so much translations as they are heightened renderings or readings of poems by Montale, Aleixandre, Paz, and others. Critics offer even less commentary regarding these poems, perhaps lacking the requisite knowledge of French, German, or Chinese that would enable them to understand the nature of Dickey's translation practices. Baughman (1985) simply observes that in these poems Dickey's voice merges with that of other poets, and while calling these efforts "noteworthy" (130), he believes the works in the volume's first section "more significant" (130).

Zweig (1980) views *The Strength of Fields* favorably, noting the "willfully eccentric" rhythms and "muscular, excessive imagery" (6) that identify Dickey. So, too, do the themes: the poems about the Second World War in general and fighter planes in particular, the "tongue-in-cheek redneck poems," and those of "grandiose escape" (6). The best poems, "The Rain Guitar," "The Strength of Fields," and "Exchanges," possess a convincing, meditative tone; the worst efforts are "swamped in language" (17). Mason (1980-81) also considers *The Strength of Fields* a good volume, containing "Dickey's best work since *Buckdancer's Choice* (1965) and 'May Day Sermon ... (1967)'" (107). "Root-Light, or the Lawyer's Daughter," "Remnant Water," and "False Youth: Autumn: Clothes of the Age" are "welcome additions" (107) to his Southern regional poems. "The Strength of Fields," a social poem as much about Dickey himself as Jimmy Carter, constitutes a meditation on what one can publicly offer the world. Among the war poems included, "Haunting the Maneuvers" is distinctive for its humor. Mason, moreover, cites "Exchanges" as a major poem because in combining his lines with those of Trumbull Stickney, Dickey conceives a work that is "ecological elegy, love lyric, meditation on death and on the relation of the poet to such social evils as oil spills" (108).

By contrast, Peters (1980) condemns most of *The Strength of Fields* for exhibiting what he labels "Momentosity" (160), Dickey's tendency to impose an unjustified sense of significance on the poems, an "easy metaphysics" (160). In additon, they contain a sentimentality that results from his affection for the subject. Peters suggests that the failure of the volume itself, which he calls "a deterioration in his work" (166), owes to the tendency of poets to view themselves as legislators and the need to keep publishing. Only "The Voyage of the Needle" and "False Youth: Autumn: Clothes of the Age" are unqualifyingly good poems because they avoid metaphysical abstractions and a false or unearned sentimentality.

Against Zweig and Peters, Dave Smith (1981) provides a balanced assessment. The poems reveal a continuation of Dickey's "obsessive and linking image patterns" (353), including those of water, flight, evasion, ascent and descent, ghosts, and animals, though the exchange with some opposite is largely absent. Moreover, his focus is more decidedly social and the enhancement of the persona derives from "sexual epiphanies and the dangers of war" (353). Smith believes that while Dickey's affirmative vision remains integral to his poems, a sense of despair evidences itself, a condition which accounts for what he discerns as a "pattern of oscillation" (353) in the poetry, a movement from connection and resolution to fear and hopelessness, or what Smith refers to as comedic joy and tragic anguish (354). The persona in the title poem sees beyond surface realities to declare his faith in the earth; in so doing, he redeems mankind (354). However, the other poems in the opening section only "aspire ... to acts of redemption" (354) through words designed to enlarge understanding of love, nature, and war. The best poems are "False Youth: Autumn: Clothes of the Age" and "Exchanges," the latter of which presents not the transformations Dickey makes in his early motion but rather a contrast between "what we give and are given of value in our lives" (354). Other poems like "For the Running of the New York Marathon" and "For the Death of Lombardi" are demonstrably weak. Yet Smith concludes that *The Strength of Fields* succeeds because Dickey brings readers "our most deeply longed for lives" (357) even as the poetry reveals a deeper awareness of death, a lessened impatience with the limitations of form, and a joy that results from simply confronting darkness with a large, visionary personality.

Baughman's (1985) discussion provides the most extensive critique of the volume, declaring that its gentle tone of acceptance and kindness shows the extent to which Dickey's psychic healing process, his re-orientation following the devastation of World War II, has succeeded. The lone family poem, "The Voyage of the Needle," dramatizes the proximity of the living and the dead and how small, almost insignificant details bring them together to show, not a combination of love and guilt as in earlier poems, but "a mended wholeness" (131). "Haunting the Maneuvers" and "Drums Where I Live," the two poems that Dickey combines in "Two Poems of the Military," and "Camden Town" and "Reunioning Dialogue," united in "Two Poems of Flight Sleep," also reveal a tone of acceptance. Death remains a concern in the war poems, but Dickey seems reconciled to its presence. Other poems attempt to establish connections, like "The Rain Guitar," which depicts renewal on the basis of shared experiences and attitudes, and "Remnant Water," the volume's most important nature poem, where the speaker confronts his fate without abandoning his purpose. Yet like Calhoun and Hill, Baughman sees the title poem as indicative of poetic intent: "More kindness will do nothing less / Than save every sleeping one / And night-walking one of us." It depicts not only the speaker's rites of passage as he learns how to "penetrate and find the source / Of the power" but also those of the people he serves and of Dickey himself. In volume after volume he consistently explores aspects of survivorship, penetrates these concerns, and achieves a renewed self. As he concludes in "The Strength of Fields," "My life belongs to the world. I will do what I can."

Critical commentary on the book's second half, "Head-Deep in Strange Sounds," remains scant and divided. Mason (1980-81) argues that with the exception of "Undersea Fragment in Colons" and "Mexican Valley," these poems illustrate the dangers of using poetic subjects unrelated to one's personal experiences and the problems of the short poem for a writer such as Dickey, "a poet of space and expansiveness" (108). Zweig (1980) declares that they are neither originals nor translations but rather more like "variations on a theme" (17) by foreign poets. Despite some successes, the section is disappointing because in changing languages Dickey often loses subtle shifts in tone and irony. His poems consequently seem "shapeless and inflated" (17). However, Peters (1981) views these "improvisations" as special, what he calls "a mixed engineering" (159), and recommends their reading. Lieberman (1980) believes these "translations" (lxv) break new ground and, unlike Zweig, sees "a wizardry of infinitesimal shifts and adjustments" (lxv), which he likens to atomic exchanges between two metals. Line and stanzaic pattern become less important here because Dickey's use of his gapped word clusters hints at "the ... magical interlocking of two voices, two languages" (ivx). Dave Smith (1981) observes that while some efforts like "Three Poems with Yevtushenko" seem near-translations, others are not even that, though all depict Dickey's theme of "the heroic Energized Man" (356). The style of these poems is radically dissimilar to that of Dickey's own work, the lines spatially dispersed, terse, and dotted with image clusters, such that each piece "feels like a parable but is not" (356). They are instead "a kind of nakedly psychic speech" (356) anticipated by *The Zodiac*.

In the preface to *The Central Motion* (1983), where these "translations" were collected, Dickey comments on his technical experimentation with foreign poets, declaring that the confrontation with the original texts results in

> the creation of a third entry that ... comes to exist by means of intuitive and improvisational powers not employed in the original, arriving out of misreadings, substitutions, leaps, absurdities, wrenchings, embarrassments, and standing at last on its own, by virtue of its own characteristics. (vii)

It is apparent that in efforts of this kind Dickey never intends to present a mere translation or copy but rather the creation of a new poem, arising from the old but with its own unique vitality and sensibility. The process of such a poem is whatever it is; the importance lies in its poetic thrust, or what he calls its "untoward glow ... arrived-at no matter how" (vii). Dickey's interest in these creations does not end with *The Strength of Fields*. His most recent volume, *The Eagle's Mile* (1990), similarly contains a section titled "Double-Tongue: Collaborations and Rewrites."

5: Return: *Puella* and *The Eagle's Mile*

As a long poem that utilizes uneven margins, varied line lengths, and gapped lines, *The Zodiac* extends the block technique Dickey first uses in poems like "Falling" and "Slave Quarters." The modified format reflects either the way the mind itself thinks, with words or phrases grouped in associational clusters, or the speech pattern of the persona or narrator, the spaces serving as natural breath pauses. The poem's book-length format and its "misreading" of Barnouw's translation of Marsman's poem continue Dickey's interest in poetic experimentation. This concern also appears in the "Head-Deep in Strange Sounds" section of *The Strength of Fields*, a volume which generally depicts the quiet gathering of his interests, talents, and techniques. The tone is kinder; Dickey's thematic concerns, more social. While the lyric impulse that characterizes the early motion yields to narrative in his central motion, the sense of guilt, the search for ideal forms, and the desire for exchange with some other being all disappear. Moreover, the poems in *The Strength of Fields* also begin to present a kind of emotional or psychological complex, the gapped spacings suggesting a suspended state of consciousness or being. The central motion, containing such metrically different poems as "The Eye-Beaters," "Pine," "The Zodiac," "Remnant Water," and "The Voyage of the Needle," now assumes another direction. Best anticipated by "Pine," it seeks to evince on the printed page a feeling of balance, the way limbs project off a main bole to suggest centrality and a sense of swaying and precariousness. Though hidden, the principal idea is nevertheless present.

Puella (1982), the beginning of Dickey's most recent motion, is the first sustained effort at what he calls in his 1983 address, "The G.I. Can of Beets, The Fox in the Wave, and The Hammers over Open Ground," "Magic-Language." For "Magicians," one of two kinds of poets, he declares,

> language itself must be paramount.... The words are seen as illuminations mainly of one another; their light of meaning plays back and forth between them, and, though it must by nature refer beyond, outside itself, shimmers back off the external world in a way whereby the world—or objective reality, or just Reality—serves as a kind of secondary necessity, a non-verbal backdrop to highlight the dance of words and their bemused interplay. (*Night Hurdling* 126-27)

Among the practitioners of this approach are Hopkins, Hart Crane, Stevens, Berryman, Mallarme, Valery, and such surrealist or surrealist-influenced poets as Paul Eluard, Frederico Garcia Lorca, and Octavio Paz. With *Puella* and *The Eagle's Mile* (1990), the lyric impulse strongly reasserts itself. The poems are related through a series of interconnected images that thread through each work, and reality becomes offered through simultaneous, intuited associations that involve these images and evoke the speaker's psychological and emotional complex. Dickey now moves distinctly into poems that reveal new techniques and yet also display a return to earlier but now re-invented forms, including narrative situations and split lines.

Van Ness (1989) sees *Puella* as Dickey's full statement of the idealization of mortal women, a theme evidenced in early poems like "Into the Stone," "Mary Sheffield," "The Leap," "The Fiend," and "Falling." The book's pointed epigraph, T. Sturge Moore's lines, "I lived in thee, and dreamed, and waked / Twice what I had been," suggests his belief in woman as a source of life-enhancing possibilities. More important, however, *Puella* attempts to present his wife Deborah's girlhood "male-imagined." Taken together, the poems trace her maturation and reveal her heightened consciousness of the world, including her kinship with the elements of fire, air, earth, and water, and her growing knowledge of human relationships. The first-person point of view in lyric poems that only in composite yield any real sense of "story," along with a technique that offers reality through intuited images or associations, gives the book a psychological depth and richness not derived from Dickey's previous narrative methods. The involved technique is important, for the images Deborah conveys evoke an emotional complex inherent in certain narrative points in time that increasingly seem timeless, that is to say, mythical, presenting the simultaneous penetration of worlds—female and male, present and past, transcendent and physical.

Dickey's tendency toward mysticism, detailed by Kirschten (1988) but earlier discussed less thoroughly and more pejoratively by Silverstein (1973), also becomes most apparent in *Puella*. Silverstein's criticism, that Dickey's "affection for metaphysics" (264), coupled with his desire for "suburban adventure" (264), too often inclines to the absurd rather than the sublime unless substantiated by a "systematic religion" (264), has proponents, including Wendell Berry (1964). Silverstein faults Dickey's efforts to capture and portray mystical transcendence, which often results merely in "a questionable luminosity" that encourages in the reader a "belief in mystery" (263). Only in *The Eye-Beaters* do poems like "In the Pocket" appear that effectively avoid joining "the trivial and the sublime" (268). However, *Puella* exalts the mystery by viewing Deborah as an archetype, imaginatively tracing her unfolding consciousness until at the volume's conclusion she becomes the environment itself. In "The Surround," which begins, "Still-down on all sides / from all over: / Dusk: seizure, quell, and hyper-glow," woman becomes a sustaining religion. Balakian (1983) sees the book as another example of Dickey's involvement with and empathy for life's otherness, but *Puella* marks an advance because it needs to be read as a single long poem in order to witness the transformative process of the persona from girl to woman. Calling the experiences "a journey," Balakian sees the poems as "a large monologue" (142) where male and female finally come together, united at the conclusion in "a celebration of marriage" (142) by the procreative powers of the female principle. The form of these poems indicates a Whitmanesque affirmation and ambitiousness, the long, expansive lines suggesting not simply the outline of an entire mind but "the pressures of the psyche, body, and spirit striving for transcendence" (143). The extended line and three-space break, which resembles an emphatic, breath-stop caesura, duplicate the dynamic processes which are the focus of *Puella*. Moreover, the linguistic qualities—the compound nouns and heavily stressed lines—correspond to something "deeply visceral" (143) in Dickey himself. Exposing these qualities and bringing them into contact with the natural rhythms of Nature enable him to impart enhanced experiences, life at the "higher frequencies" (143).

Puella opens with a rite of initiation. In "Deborah Burning a Doll Made of House-Wood," Deborah burns her past and journeys into time, still very much innocent but wanting to accumulate the power within mortal life: "I level / Stay level / and kneel and disappear slowly / Into Time, as you, with sun-center force / take up the house / In Hell-roaring steps, a Heaven-beaming holocaust." The purgation of her old self, symbolized by the doll, begins her new life in "Deborah, Moon, Mirror, Right Hand Rising." Seeing in her mirror a reflection of the moon as it shines through the window, Deborah realizes her change: "Woman of the child / I was, I am shone-through now / In circles, as though the moon in my hand were falling / Concentrically, on the spirit of a tree." "Deborah in Ancient Lingerie, In Twin Oak over Creek" shows the persona finding the mythic sources of life, a reclamation of Edenic strength, so that she becomes "a kind of protean goddess straining the shapes into the visible and invisible world" (Balakian 143). Because she possesses phylogenetic and ontogenetic qualities like Roethke's lost son, Dickey's girl reveals a racial memory. In poems such as "Springhouse, Menses, Held Apple, House and Beyond" and "Deborah as Scion," she assumes the blood of all women, and nature becomes "God-charged in a Hopkinsean way" (144). "The Lyric Beasts," where Deborah releases herself "in hounded flame-outs, stalling and renewing," and "The Surround," where she enlarges her power to become the "Environment," continue and complete her growth and fulfillment. In presenting "the history of a soul" (145) and the transformation of a man into new life, Dickey extends aspects of Whitman, Hopkins, and Roethke to reveal his belief in "the passional act of struggle" (145).

Spears (1987) asserts that while the poems in *Puella* are personal, they nonetheless display a formality, or "folk ceremoniousness" (120), toward the subject, and the verse itself reveals a Hopkinsean tenderness opening to the beauty of the world. Some of these folk-ceremony poems, including "Deborah and Deidre as Drunk Bridesmaids Footracing at Daybreak," "Veer-Voices: Two Sisters under Crows," and "Deborah in ·Ancient Lingerie, In Thin Oak over Creek," suggest a playfulness completely different from that of "May Day Sermon," as when in the last of these, Deborah thinks: "Right over you, I can do / at no great height I can do / and bear / And counter-balance and do / and half-sway and do / and sway / and outsway and / do." The influence of Hopkins appears in "Heraldic: Deborah and Horse in Morning Forest," which offers an epigraph from the poet, and "From Time," where Deborah's piano playing is conveyed with Hopkins's verse techniques. Spears declares that the sequence of poems moves from the realism of "Deborah as Scion" to the visionary in "The Lyric Beasts," from Deborah recognizing the attributes she has inherited from past ancestors to her becoming a goddess urging her followers to "Rise and on faith / Follow." The poems, moreover, reveal distinctly Southern qualities, such as a stress on place; the sense of communal myth that shows a love of ritual and ceremony, particularly in the family; humor in the form of an outlandish lie or impossible vision which shocks but then manifests a deeper truth; and a strong, religious feeling in poems that are often sermons, prayers, or invocations and which display a creed so fundamental that it concerns man's relationship to all life (122). *Puella* presents a vision distinctly different from the cosmic influences of *The Zodiac* in that its concern is the domestic world, where the persona, "the daughter-wife" (123), displays a gentleness and humor and the verse assumes a "formal musicality" (123). While noting that the speaker is a Jungian anima-figure, Spears pointedly avoids assessing whether the source of joy within these poems derives from a newly integrated personality of Dickey himself.

Dickey has assisted in resurrecting the poetic persona, what he calls in *Sorties* the "I-figure" (155), who almost disappeared in the modernist fragmentation of self and in its self-directed irony. While he has achieved a larger-than-life reputation, he has generally avoided becoming completely identified with his speakers. Rather, he conveys the impression that his experiences are universal, and his poetic discoveries have seemed to surprise even himself. Applewhite (1985) believes the speaker in his poems, after Dickey has provisionally identified him or her, is then called to by "a deeper-lying stratum of his being" (214) because Dickey deliberately struggles to lose himself in language. This decidedly romantic loss mandates the discovery of a larger, more central understanding. For example, "Root-Light, or the Lawyer's Daughter" from *The Strength of Fields* shows the young woman becoming a part of the river. To extend that portrayal would involve feeling through her senses, which is what *Puella* accomplishes. In "Veer-Voices: Two Sisters under Crows," Dickey's male identity becomes transformed, split, mirrored, and then redoubled. One sister, Deborah, nears the identity of the other, where both represent "the human tensions" (215) as they are voiced by the veering cries of crows. Like Spears, Applewhite discerns a progression in the poems, a "core of psychological process" (216). Early poems depict Deborah realizing her individuality, once by means of her reflection in "Deborah, Moon, Mirror, Right Hand Rising," where the sight in a mirror of self with the moon initiates the relationship with the natural world. The opening poem, "Deborah Burning a Doll Made of House-Wood," dramatizes the child's "apocalyptic tendency" (216) to oppose this world. However, Applewhite sees a dialectic, the girl's desire to negate the world (and so manifest her "power to see / Pure loss") countered by an attitude suggesting the adult need for structures, her love of carpenters and their "God-balanced bubbles." This dialectic results in the girl's learning to express herself through the things about her, such as the cries of crows in "Veer-Voices" and later through horseback riding and the arrival of menstruation. In "Ray-Flowers," Deborah falls into the world from "some center of self-contained spiritual identity" (216) that still opposes limitations. Using sensory illusion, Dickey then shows her awakening, curious about the world, in "Heraldic: Deborah and Horse in Morning Forest," where the rapid flux of phenomena as she rides counters her figurative blindness. Motion physically present, while threatening the loss of self, finally serves to reassert order and understanding as the poet and his persona transcend the world as process.

Calhoun and Hill's (1983) brief examination of *Puella* centers on its poetic techniques, including the use of compound words, a reliance upon fragmented images to render simultaneity, an unusual syntax and oddly musical tones to suggest a new sense of the world, and a "metaphysical shift" (106) toward a transcendent world where a larger unity subsumes perceived differences and peculiarities. While the poems concern a girl's maturation into womanhood, they are also "an exercise in language" (106), particularly using participles, as if by such means words might become the thing itself. When he writes of "The whole mingling oversouling loom / Of this generation," Dickey assumes an Emersonian attitude, but the technique risks reader accessibility as he struggles for otherness that is "wide-open collisionless color of the whole night / Ringed-in, pure surface."

Baughman (1985) argues that the organization of *Puella* reveals not a progression, as Spears (1987) and Applewhite (1985) assert, but a pattern of imagery that involves the elements of fire, air, water, and earth and images of sound. These evoke emotional response and cause reader participation. "Deborah Burning a Doll Made of House-Wood" and "Doorstep, Lightning, Waif-Dreaming" involve fire, the former a ritual destruction and baptism announcing her coming of age and the latter a declaration that she is "a creature born from intense lightning" (137) who possesses a "root-system of fire." The girl's association with earth appears in "Ray-Flowers (I)" and "Ray-Flowers (II)," where she spirals to earth to become transformed from seeds to "equalling / Spirits of land." In addition, "Deborah as Scion" shows a connection with the earth as she visits her ancestors' graves. "The Lode," which is subtitled "Deborah's Rain-Longing," and "Deborah in Mountain Sound: Bell, Glacier, Rose" use water to suggest the speaker's increasing sexuality. This latter poem also shows Dickey's method of lyrical indirectness. The bell's sound is never explicitly presented; rather, the sound evokes an image of itself, as when Dickey describes one of its notes as "space-thinning   space-harvesting metal— / ... Life-longing intervals ... / Reasonless as cloud." The thematic conclusion of the volume occurs in "The Surround," spoken to James Wright as he moves from life to death. Baughman argues that in addition to showing Deborah's final incarnation as the environment, the poem unites all the important images: the reflected echo of veer-sounds, the circles and rings that mirror the cycle of life and death, and the unity of fire, air, water, and earth. Along with *The Zodiac* and *The Strength of Fields*, *Puella* reveals "new voices and new tones" (143) and completes Dickey's psychological recovery from the Second World War, though his tendency to risk language poetically implies that other effects will follow.

Hollahan (1985) traces the origins of *Puella* to Dickey's interest in Hopkins's *The Wreck of the "Deutschland."* Attempting to counter perceived images of "'red-neck' grossness" (2) about himself and his work, Dickey undertook to write particularly modern poems. Though he does not argue a deliberate effort to manipulate popular and critical assessment as does Bowers (1985), Hollahan does state that Hopkins's poem became Dickey's model and, using Harold Bloom's concept concerning the "anxiety of influence" (2), that Dickey overcame any apprehension about doing so and successfully adopted the influence. While depicting a girl's transition into womanhood, a passage with much socio-psychological relevancy today, *Puella* possesses a deeper purpose indicated both by the epigraph to Rilke, whose lyric poems of rich, symbolic images sought a mystical unity with God, and by the Hopkinsean attitude that poetry should remove itself from prose through verbal play, lively melody, unusual words, and word-compounds. While the girl in *Puella* is Deborah, she is also "the muse of poetry" (4), and the volume's difficult, sometimes inaccessible language owes to Dickey's effort to accommodate Rilke's view of the poet and Hopkins's attitude toward language, in particular the latter's long poem about the drowning of five Franciscan nuns. In his criticism of a 1971 trade edition printing of the poem by the Boston publishing house of David Godine, Dickey writes in part: "here, at long last, is a *complete* poetry, working powerfully at all levels, at once both wild and swift beyond all other wildness and swiftness and stringently, savagely disciplined: a language *worked* for all it can give" (*Babel to Byzantium* 239). Hollahan argues that this three-page introduction "functions as a mediation" (8) between *Puella* and *The Wreck of the "Deutschland,"* two otherwise very different poems by two very different poets, and he notes a number of important similarities: diction that resembles Hopkins's, run-on syntax or sprung rhythm, a Hopkinsean thematics, Hopkins's eight-line stanza, his sea storm, and his insistence on instress as existential essence (9-11). Moreover, Hopkins's voice blends with that of the Tall Nun just as Dickey's voice becomes indistinguishable from Deborah's. Hollahan believes that Hopkins's rapid flow of language, his view of a total poetry that embraces all parochial elements, his belief in nature as "a Kantian-Hegalian complex surrounding mankind" (12), his desperate uniqueness, and his effort to shape a "disciplined outpour" (12) all assisted Dickey in fashioning a poetry more modern than his previous efforts.

Technically and thematically, *The Eagle's Mile* (1990) constitutes a culmination of Dickey's poetic journey, an extension of *Puella* in one sense and a return to poetic elements apparent in the early motion in another. In

"The G.I. Can of Beets, The Fox in the Wave, and The Hammers over Open Ground," Dickey expresses reservations about the use of "Magic-Language." Acknowledging that he is not a magic-language practitioner, he nevertheless admits to having recently worked with that side of language. Consequently, he has become conscious "of ranges of expression, of possibilities, of departures, of 'new thresholds, new anatomies,' that I previously had no idea existed" (*Night Hurdling* 133). Yet such poems cannot achieve greatness, he argues, because "they cannot *build*.... They have no armature: of narrative, of logic, of idea-development and/or succession or change, or transformation; they are not thematic, or at least the theme is most of the time not publicly available" (137). By having *Puella* read as one long poem, Dickey attempts to create or provide an armature the nature of which has been variously critiqued. Applewhite (1985) and Spears (1987) offer an chronological or spatial interpretation, and Baughman (1985) presents an imagistic analysis. Yet the highly elevated language, while effecting a heightened emotional experience, also lessens reader accessibility, denying him the narrative means by which to enter the experience, an immediate sense of place and action which *Puella* only obliquely provides. Poetry which does offer such specifics is practiced by those who oppose "Magic-Language," what Dickey labels the "Commentary-on-Life party, the Human Conditioners" (126), who are in some sense, in many senses, "literalists." These include Homer, Frost, Robinson, Masters, Hardy, Francis Ponge and Guilleric in France, the early Gottfried in Germany, Philip Larkin and R.S. Thomas in England, and perhaps the prime example, Randall Jarrell. These writers use plain words in straightforward order to make a statement, most often about something that happened to someone or the condition of the happening. Their language does not call attention to itself but, like a clear pane of glass, offers a circumstance cleanly. When Dickey closes "The G.I. Can of Beets," he admits to being profoundly interested in what might be made to yield if these two opposite approaches to language were somehow intertwined "to make metaphors I have never yet been able to achieve, bound into one poetic situation, one scene, one event after another" (139). The effort to discover this ideal form or netting by combining the strongest threads of the present two kinds, thereby giving the mind its absolute freedom but within the poet's own, imposed, formal limits—this has become Dickey's present search.

What has changed for Dickey over his poetic career is not the nature of what he wants; he has always seemed to know his principal concern. Simply stated, he has hunted not *a* but *the* central situation, *the* general theme. His criticism of the poems of other artists can often be reduced to one fault—their terrible inconsequentiality because they lack the world, its inexplicable, marvelous creation and its strange, spell-casting fullness, in the midst of which is the naked human response. He clearly states the nature and function of poetry in his essay "Metaphor as Pure Adventure." "I think of the poem," he asserts, as a kind of action in which, if the poet can participate *enough*, other people cannot help participating as well. I am against all marmoreal, closed, to-be-contemplated kinds of poems and conceive of the poem as a minute part of the Heraclitean flux, and of the object of the poem as not to slow or fix or limit the flux at all but to try as it can to preserve and implement the "fluxness," the flow, and show this moving through the poem, coming in at the beginning and going back out, after the end, into the larger, nonverbal universe whence it came. (*Sorties* 173-74)

Rather than for any contemporary idea or topical concern, Dickey searches for the basic human act and for the proper net or form by which the poet allows the experience to show itself. The making of this net, the use of metaphor and image to hold the experience and reveal its essential wonder so that the world might be individually re-discovered—this remains Dickey's intent. It cannot be accomplished neatly but needs not only force and abandon, what he calls "verbal *velocity*" (*Sorties* 57), but also a deep clarity. *The Eagle's Mile* is Dickey's effort to create this new form. In doing so, he returns to certain elements present in his early poetry. Together with *Puella*, the volume constitutes Dickey's late motion, the final complement to his collected poetry, *The Whole Motion*, due to be published in 1992.

Mitgang's (1990) review sees in *The Eagle's Mile* a continuation of Dickey's examination of man's connection with nature, a relationship that includes "many nuances about myth and machismo" (16). The language "meanders down the page in rivulets" that finally come together in "a rushing mainstream" (16) which includes linked words and startling phrases. Together these linguistic devices extend "his vision" (16). Mitgang, however, does not identify the first of these qualities as a variation of the block format most evident in Dickey's central motion or the latter as a continuation of the language in *Puella*, nor does he explain the precise meaning behind "vision." Chappell's (1990) overview centers on the quality of diction and syntax. Noting that the poet's reputation derives from his strong narrative, Chappell declares that *The Eagle's Mile* constitutes strikingly different work, an idiom he labels as "the High Bardic, the vatic, the transcendent—the Pindaric Grandiose" (5F) and defines as "heroic visionary ambitions marching out to trample the limitations of ordinary poetic diction" (5F). It resembles Hopkins in tone and often results in what Chappell calls an "intoxicated grandeur" (5F). Yet *The Eagle's Mile* suffers from certain flaws, including overstated language ("I, oversouling for an instant // With them"), banality ("God-father, I say // To him: not father of God, but assistant / Father to this one"), bathos (the sea as "Up front for all of us"), slang ("I speak to you from where / I was shook off"), farfetched tropes ("play-penned / With holocaust"), disingenious direct address ("Oh fire, come on! I trust you!"), the overuse of "blindside" and the outdated preposition "amongst," and an insistence on gerunds.

The most thorough critical analysis is Van Ness's essay "'Up from the human down-beat': Double-Vision and Elemental Complicity in James Dickey's *The Eagle's Mile*," which appears in the G.K. Hall *Critical Essays* series. The volume's title poem has as its epigraph William Blake's line, "The Emmet's Inch & Eagle's Mile," and is strategically centered to reflect the book's thematic arrangement. The poem juxtaposes the two points of view that dominate the overall work: the ideal, sweeping gaze of an eagle in flight and the limited stare of a man walking on the ground. The persona, as he first imaginatively rises with the bird "receiving overlook" and later as he stands on the shoreline "foreseeing / Around a curve," understands these perspectives as important to learning "the circular truth" of the world. Each poem in *The Eagle's Mile* depicts a singular experience or stance, and each is linked to others by patterns of imagery which reveal the complexion of physical reality, its "basic elemental complicity or connection." Because the speaker arrives at an intuitive understanding of life, he achieves a "double-vision or view" and knows that both the eagle's mile and the emmet's inch discern the truth of this world.

The Eagle's Mile manifests elements from all of Dickey's previous techniques. The poems not only present a narrative situation reminiscent of his early work, although the action usually remains static, but they also exhibit the spacings or interstices of the split-line technique. Dickey utilizes the block format only in "The Olympian," and this is slightly modified. Frequently, the poems appear balanced on the page with the lines symmetrically branching off a central idea. Yet unlike any previous volume, Dickey thematically relates the poems through a series of interconnected images that thread through the work. While *Puella* captures the individual moments in a girl's life as she matures, uniting the poems which depict her emotional and physical states through their narrative points in time and emphasizing her elemental connections, *The Eagle's Mile* links many separate images, including those of grass or weeds; graves; footprints; rocks; birds; the elements of air, water, and earth; curves or curving; and climatic heat and cold. All life, Dickey implies, is fundamentally connected at all times. In addition, while he joins with these poems a series of others entitled "Double-Tongue: Collaborations and Re-writes," which reveal similar themes, the principal poems, beginning with "Eagles," move first from those centering on the persona's identification with Nature, to those depicting essential human relationships, before finally returning to the physical realm in "Expanses." Here the speaker feels the emotion of "Joy like short grass," an attitude whose image unites both life and death. The poems therefore trace a journey, one unconsciously undertaken; halfway through these is the book's center, the title poem.

That search begins with "Eagles," which establishes Dickey's grounding principle by insisting upon the inability of the individual ever to escape the world fully enough to gain complete understanding of it. The speaker imaginatively conceives himself lifted by the feet of an eagle. He is a man "who, for twenty lines / Of a new poem, thought he would not be shut /

From those wings." In the poems that follow, Dickey's persona confronts his own limitations, as in "Gila Bend" where he observes: "You should brand, brand / The ground but you don't." He then proceeds toward an emotional comprehension of nature, first through abandoning his eyesight in "Night Bird," where he understands "there is no limit / To what a man can get out of / his failure to see," and later in "Immortals," where he individually confronts the elements of air, water, and earth. In other poems such as "The One," "The Three," and "The Six," he discovers "the principled physical relevance of *things* individual or together" as well as the "situational importance they assume at special moments of heightened awareness." Eventually, the persona realizes that the panoramic sweep of the eagle's gaze and the restricted view of the emmet reach the same understanding. For example, in "Circuits" he walks the shore and senses that beaches tend toward completion: "As they ram and pack, foreseeing / Around a curve, always   slow-going headlong / For the circle / ... their minds on a perfect connection, no matter / How long it takes." Such knowledge "will hit you / Straight out of the wind, on wings or not, / Where you have blanked yourself / Still with your feet." Only after entering nature intuitively does Dickey's speaker confront death.

In a series of poems that focus on mortality, including "The Olympian," "Sleepers," "Tomb Stone," and "To Be Done in Winter," the persona recognizes that the reality of death demands a life of consequence. Human companionship lessens isolation, and in "Daughter," "The Little More," and "For a Time and Place," Dickey celebrates the coming and continuation of life. Finally, returning once more to nature in "Snow Thickets," he knows not only that one needs the dual vision offerred by poetic inspiration but that "the physical forces governing the world must be countered with upthrust, the opposite but essential human response." In the final poem, "Expanses," gazing now with the eagle at a man who might be himself, he surveys the broader, geographic arena to discover "boundless, / Earthbound, trouble-free, and all you want— / Joy like short grass."

"The Eagle's Mile," centered to show the speaker moving from nature into the social world, emphasizes the need to enter the endless variety of physical creation while also recognizing one can never finally surpass it. One must always be "drawing life / From growth / From flow," knowing that like William Douglas, to whom Dickey dedicates the poem, one can at best possess only a "patched tunnel-gaze" that remains "exactly right / For the buried track." *The Eagle's Mile* demands, as Dickey writes in "For a Time and Place," that "we be able to begin with ourselves / Underfoot and rising." The book acknowledges limitations while passionately insisting that the human need to strive above one's earthbound condition is "undeniable, necessary, and redemptive." It is the elemental human condition and the beginning of the artistic process.

6: The Children's Poetry

DICKEY'S TWO CHILDREN'S BOOKS, *Tucky the Hunter* (1978) and *Bronwen, the Traw, and the Shape-Shifter* (1986), have received almost no critical study, perhaps because he has devoted so little published effort in this regard compared to other major twentieth-century poets like Randall Jarrell and Anne Sexton. Reviews are sparse, mostly superficial, and generally mixed. Both books concern the exploits of a family member, the former involving Dickey's grandson, James Bayard Tuckerman Dickey, and the latter, his daughter Bronwen Elaine. In addition, both works mythologize the adventure the protagonist undergoes, a larger-than-life confrontation with real or imagined creatures.

Good children's poetry possesses a singing quality, a melody and motion. If the poem is mysterious, meditative, or nostalgic, the lines move slowly and the words become subtle. Language is exact and descriptive as well as sensory and connotative. While such poetry displays a strong emotional resonance, its foundation lies in ideas; therefore, it also appeals to the intellect, often taking everyday facts of life and giving them new meaning or showing the strange and extraordinary as safe and even life-enhancing. Whatever the experience presented, it must exhibit an arresting significance. Illustrations are not only comprehensible but also evoke emotional identification, allowing for the large exercise of the reader's imagination and an intense personal response. Like the text, they provide a vital, wholesome perspective by which to understand life. Taken together, words and pictures constitute an integrated, complex work of visual art, with each aspect creating conditions of dependence and interdependence. The text and the illustrations cohere and complement one another such that the book's format and layout are, finally, an aesthetic, psychological, and intellectual consideration.

Tucky the Hunter and *Bronwen, the Traw, and the Shape-Shifter* exhibit certain of these qualities, but each is flawed. *Bronwen*, which Dickey labels "A Poem in Four Parts," is the more complex in character and plot, the more dramatic, and the more likely to intrigue both adults and children. However, while the black-and-white drawings by Richard Jesse Watson are intricately detailed, they not so much complement the poem as establish a counter-claim to the reader's interest. By contrast, the pastel sketches by Marie Angel in *Tucky the Hunter* more delicately cohere with the text rather than confront it, but the plot is simple and the protagonist's adventure mostly static. With both books, reviewers failed to offer substantive analysis, their commentary often revealing only the most general knowledge of Dickey's poetic themes. Logue (1979), for instance, declares that *Tucky the Hunter* celebrates the imagination of Dickey's grandson, his "oneness with the animal kingdom and his popgun" (68), as he hunts and shoots in his bed the world's wild creatures. Angel's paintings thoroughly detail the natural world, and the collaboration of poem and paintings seems "arrested in mid-flight of fantasy" (68). Johnston (1978) considers the work another successful example of Dickey's collaborative efforts with visual artists, which has produced such books as *Jericho: The South Beheld* (1974) and *God's Images* (1977). The rhymes "trip along drolly" (88), and the water colors display "imagination and sensitivity" (88). *Kirkus Reviews* (1978) provides the most condemnatory overview, calling the verses "forgettable" (917). Unlike other critics, the reviewer compares *Tucky* with works by authors of noted children's literature, including Maurice Sendak and A.A. Milne. Dickey's subject is "suburban nighttime exploits" (917), but the book lacks Sendak's poise and the conclusion is too obvious and reassuring. *Tucky* is "kind of slippery for children, too slight for adults" (917). Angel's delicate illustrations, while striking, overwhelm the meager text, which, unlike Milne, is "mismatched to the mock-serious tone of the poem" (917). In their later bio-critical study, Calhoun and Hill (1983) discern familiar Dickey themes of hunting and a spiritual exchange with nature, citing the line, "They sang in mystic double-tongue, the tongue of man and beast." Also evident from Dickey's mature poetry is the presence of the suburbs. Because *Tucky the Hunter* offers nothing poetically innovative, Calhoun and Hill declare only that the book "seems to work" (101) with its limitations, but they neither analyze these themes nor attempt to compare their use with the mature poems.

Skinner (1979) remains the only critical essay focusing on Dickey's first children's book, though its brevity is indicative of the academic response to Dickey's efforts in this area. Tucky matures as a result of his experiences, which includes imaginary visits not only to places like Alaska, the Philippines, and Africa, but also to "the suburbs of the sun" and "the suburbs of Venus and of Mars." When Susan, Tucky's mother, comes to check on her sleeping son, he gives her the song of the meadow lark, his hunting trophy, so that she, too, participates in his adventure. The poem's "fun" (56) derives from Dickey's ability to merge into the narrative delightful sounds with periodic nonsense. Endeavoring to involve the reader, he also includes suspense: "Tucky hunted EVERYTHING / but I hope not YOU and ME!" The music, set by quatrains with an *abcb* rhyme scheme, enhances the text. Yet because each quatrain consists of two separate couplets, the poem's pace speeds up, and the rhymes become expected. Most of the first and third lines have four accented syllables; the second and fourth, three. Alliterative phrases like "At Samarkand the whirling stars all whistle wild and pale" and "he slew it for its song" contribute to the poem's musical quality. Additionally, Skinner notes Dickey's use of onomatopoeia ("snapping wolverine" and "bumbling Kodiak") and his vivid verbs that render improbable events both realistic and musically pleasing ("a grinning crocodile in the Ganges thick and brown, / gobbled up a newsboy in the middle of the town"). Such qualities broaden the poem's appeal to include adults as well as children. *Tucky the Hunter* enables children to share a boy's imaginative dreams as he discovers "his oneness with the universe and its inhabitants" (58), but adults respond to the musical qualities in the language.

The reviews of *Bronwen, the Traw, and the Shape-Shifter* are primarily negative. *Kirkus* (1986), while advising that adults would share Dickey's enjoyment in elevating his daughter into myth, also states that the poem is awkward if read aloud. The meter is "complex" and the diction "uneven" (1289), occasionally simple and childlike and at other times extended into complex images. The text's "poetic fantasy" (1289), however, is effectively portrayed by Watson's illustrations, which capture the "dark romantic tone" (1289) reminiscent of Sendak but are longer and more complicated than the latter. Whalin (1986) also criticizes the book's language. Bronwen's adventures appear in "excruciatingly lengthy detail" (173). The large, black-and-white drawings are "strong" (173) but do not mitigate the "plodding language" and "dragging action" (173). Though intended as an epic, which should have a quickened pace, *Bronwen* more often remains stationary.

Macaulay's (1987) essay-review details his objections in order to determine where specific fault lies for a work not so much an epic as "an endless poem" (31). Book one succeeds, introducing Bronwen and the All-Dark as the heroine and villain, respectively, as well as her magical traw, and moving from the sunlight and safety of the garden to the menacing shadows of Bronwen's bedroom as the All-Dark awakens. However, as the story progresses, it "flattens" (31) because imagination yields to mere acceptance. "Conventional fantasy" replaces the "power of suggestion" (31). The images that present Bronwen's battle with the All-Dark must be viewed not only in their format but also with the illustrations, and Watson's pictures reveal "the dangers of illustrating a text that already illustrates itself" (31). The drawings possess a sense of darkness but no mystery; having texture, they lack feeling. Moreover, the pictures struggle against themselves. The "star-warsian double-page spread" (31) that depicts Bronwen's battle with fire, wind, and water conflicts with the illustrations that portray the empowering of the traw. Macaulay asserts, however, that "the real battle is between words and pictures, between the imagined and the unavoidable, the suggested and the concrete" (31). Behind any successful picture book lies the integration of these opposites, but *Bronwen* becomes two books, one of words and the other of pictures, which share only the common packaging. Suggesting that its failure lies with an agent or editor who saw "a sure thing" (31) in Dickey's name and Watson's pictures, Macaulay then concludes by declaring the book "an over-designed, ill-conceived, pretentious product" (31) that undercuts the abilities of both artists.

Sporborg's (1987) lengthy review sees *Bronwen* positively, declaring that the "timeless fear of the dark" (25) inspires the book's "powerful echoic verses" (25). Bronwen's "vision-quest" (26) involves confronting the elements of fire, wind, and water; success in each instance costs her the magic in one of the traw's tines. Only when she battles "the endless black deep of the earth" and wins because the traw's handle blazes with magic power is the All-Dark finally defeated. Sporborg observes the changes in tone and poetic cadence that reflect a deepening despair as the narrative becomes more threatening. While the literal interpretation of the subject matter, together with the dedication ("To Bronwen and Her Mother in the Elements"), suggests an autobiographical content, the book speaks more openly to all readers.

7: The Poet as Novelist: *Deliverance* and *Alnilam*

CONCERNING THE PUBLICATION OF his first novel in 1970, Dickey states: "*Deliverance* is really a novel about how decent men kill, and the fact that they get away with it raises a lot of questions about staying within the law—whether decent people have the right to go outside the law when they're encountering human monsters" (Ashley 77). He adds: "I wrote *Deliverance* as a story where under the conditions of extreme violence people find out things about themselves that they would have no other means of knowing" (79). Though the fictional account of four suburbanites and their white-water trip through the rugged terrain of North Georgia was a popular best-seller, reviewers generally failed to regard it as critically significant. DeMott (1970), for example, dismisses the book as "entertaining, shoot'em-up mindlessness" (38) and an "emptily rhetorical horse-opera played in canoes" (43). Connell (1970), while acknowledging Dickey's experience with language and his ability to create and sustain dramatic tension, nevertheless believes the first-person narration raises awkward problems. Ed Gentry, who relates the adventure, murders a mountaineer, conceals the body, and lies to the sheriff; yet now in a book he recounts these experiences. Moreover, despite presenting the story in past tense, the narrator fully and sytematically remembers the dialogue. That the voice recounting the grotesque story is a complacent American businessman also strains believability.

The poetic quality of the language troubles some critics. For example, when Gentry climbs the sheer cliff in his desperate attempt to save his companions, he thinks, "With each shift to a newer and higher position I felt more and more tenderness toward the wall." Such diction, Eyster (1971) believes, reveals "the poet gone astray" (471) because mediated responses become substituted for simple terror. The prose does not inappropriately yield to the poetic, but a melodramatic situation assumes poetic significance. Dickey admits to being conscious of this possibility during the novel's composition:

> *Deliverance* was originally written in a very heavily charged prose, somewhat reminiscent of James Agee. But it was too juicy. It distracted from the narrative thrust, which is the main thing that the story has going for it. So I spent two or three drafts taking that quality out. I wanted a kind of unobtrusively remarkable observation that wouldn't call attention to itself. That's why I made the narrator an art director. He's a guy who *would* see things like this; a writer would perform all kinds of cakewalks to be brilliant stylistically,

which would have interfered with the narrative drive of the story.
(Ashley 77)

The poetic texture of the prose also derives from Dickey's use of similar
material in previously published poems like "On the Coosawattee," events
and circumstances that "I was trying to reconceive in terms of the novel"
(78). This descriptive language, while raising *Deliverance* above the level of
an escapist adventure to what Eyster calls "a modern Gothic horror story"
(470), also places it in a larger tradition of heroic, epical struggles that
includes the *Odyssey*, Conrad's *Heart of Darkness*, and Crane's "The Open
Boat" (470).

Yet Eyster also faults the novel's celebration of male bravado and
message of macho fitness. In attempting to achieve thematic as well as
stylistic significance, Dickey fails to establish the "moral values of terror and
violence" (470) where killer and victim become ambivalently connected.
Dependent upon one another, they perform together "a ritual of salvation
through sacrifice" (470). This failure results from what Eyster believes is
Dickey's simplistic personal philosophy as to the nature and function of
violence and from his depiction of stereotypes. Ed Gentry, Bobby Trippe,
and Drew Ballinger are "interchangeable and indistinguishable" (471), and
Lewis Medlock offers little new as a modern descendent of Natty Bumppo.
Simply stated, the characters are "humdrum" (471), an evaluation which
explains why the novel's larger moral questions remain unanswered. This
lack of complexity particularly disturbs Eyster, who concludes that Dickey's
"vision of life cannot even exist except when it is confined to the animal
world, to the world of sub-humans, or to stock outdoor characters" (471).
Deliverance, consequently, becomes mere artificiality.

Other critics see in the novel the deliberate use of myth as it involves a
ritualistic initiation and rebirth. Specifically, Dickey incorporates elements
of the rites of passage to return to primitive but enhanced states of being. As
an influence he points to a review by Stanley Edgar Hyman in the summer
1949 issue of the *Kenyon Review* where Hyman quotes from Arnold Van
Gennep's "rites de passage" and cites "a separation from the world, a
penetration to some source of power, and a life-enhancing return" (Arnett
295). The book's structure, consisting of a "Before" and "After" section
between which Dickey narrates the events of September 14, 15, and 16,
reinforces the mythic infrastructure. During their journey, the four suburban-
ites leave their safe, middle-class domesticity and enter the larger world of
nature, an intimacy that reveals forgotten or unknown truths to them. This
connection, evident in all Dickey's writings, is a relationship he personally
respects and even mandates, declaring in *Self-Interviews* that "I'm like
Thoreau in this respect. He had great knowledge—much greater than
mine—of the natural world and a great intimacy with it. I don't think
knowledge precludes this kind of intimacy" (68). The effort to retrieve a
sense of communion, a vicarious re-enactment of primate man's essential

affinity with nature, evidences itself in poems like "Springer Mountain" but becomes most fully explored in *Deliverance*.

The transformation is accomplished through the river. Becoming the agent of change, it carries the four men deep into the rugged wilds and into human nature. With its numinous presence, constantly changing its aspects, it assumes the existence of what Guillory (1976) calls "a god-in-the-object" (57). It is not simply that every major action occurs either on, in, or near the river but rather that it exerts an atavistic power and influence. At once almost mindful and mindless of the canoeists, the river maintains a primal authority and elemental sacredness throughout *Deliverance*. Hanging from the sheer side of the cliff, Gentry stares at the water below him and beholds "that terrific brightness. Only a couple of rocks as big as islands, around one of which a kind of red seemed to go, as though outlining a face, a kind of god ...." Its transcendent being reflects Dickey's own attitudes concerning a river. He states in *Self-Interviews* that it is "the most beautiful thing in nature. *Any* river" (69), and it is the river that finally delivers Gentry and the others. When Gentry descends the cliff, having killed the mountaineer, the rope breaks. Despite kicking away from the precipice, he lives only because he lands in the river. Then, too, the river hides Stovall's body, and when in the last series of rapids the canoeists are sucked through a rocky channel, the canoe shoots above the churning water and lands in a clear pool. Six weeks later, the Cahulawassee, now dammed, floods its banks and obliterates all evidence of the experiences; but because it also possesses an "immanent meaning" (58), the river leaves on Gentry's psyche a lasting impression. His view of himself and the world alters. He re-evaluates daily activities, thinking: "And so it ended, except in my mind, which changed the events more deeply into what they were, into what they meant to me alone."

Guillory, however, sees the novel's mythic aspects as more than simply a structural parallel to the heroic journey. Because Gentry's exploits occur on a mythic scale, they qualify his personality and result in a "basic clarification of human values" (58). He becomes metamorphosed from a complacent, get-through-the-day businessman to a newly awakened sensibility possessing "authentic human and aesthetic motivation" (58). The woman with the golden eye furnishes a measure by which to determine the extent of his trans- formation. Initially, Gentry is "mainly interested in sliding," a man who has reduced his life and his relationships to the mechanical. He feels trapped by a sense of life's worthlessness, so the woman modeling artificial silk underwear for his ad agency seems to promise deliverance. As he later makes love to his wife, Martha, he fantasizes about the model: "The girl from the studio threw back her hair and clasped her breast, and in the center of Martha's heaving and expertly working back, the gold eye shone ... that promised other things, another life, deliverance." Gentry's experiences in the wilderness, however, where he assumes the role of hunter and acts with what Guillory labels "an ineluctable brutality" (60), change the principles by which he lives. Scaling the cliff, held by fear and a "moon-blazing sexuality," Gentry seeks "a slice of gold like the model's in the river." The transcendent experience causes him to place the woman in perspective. He thinks, "I see her every now and then, and the studio uses her. She is a pleasant part of the world, but minor. She is imaginary." Though his understanding is partly a reassessment of sex, the transformation is deeper. Guillory argues that following his epical survival on the river, Gentry experiences "the return of the alchemical powers of inspiration" (60). Stating that the river "is always finding a way to serve me," he resumes work on his collages and rehires an artist previously replaced.

Deliverance does not attack suburbia or advertising but rather examines and criticizes what Guillory labels "the self-insulating boredom that frustrates the search for human wholeness and creativity" (61). Gentry states, "The river and everything I remembered about it became a possession to me, a personal, private possession, as nothing else in my life ever had. Now it ran nowhere but in my head, and there it ran as though immortally." The river effects the return of Gentry's creative energies, retrieved from an enervated existence in one revelatory experience that constitutes for Guillory "the final human meaning in the myth of Ed Gentry's deliverance" (62). Dickey's view, then, is that redemption lies with the imagination.

Critics have variously interpreted the nature, extent, and intent of the novel's myth. Armour (1973) sees a modern representation of the archetypal hero as Adam, who confronts his adventures with native innocence. Citing R.W.B. Lewis's description in *The American Adam,* he asserts that *Deliverance* depicts "a variation of the pattern" (280) in each of the four canoeists. Returning to primitive America, they arm themselves only with knives and bows and arrows. When they capture two guns from the mountain men, they bury the shotgun and throw the rifle in the river, a sacrifice of the symbols of civilization to nature, in order that they not diminish the test of themselves. As American Adams, they must risk physical dangers that challenge their heroic capabilities and threaten their essential innocence. The river provides the most obvious dangers; rocks, falls, and rapids warn of death. Yet other men resisting invasion of their terrority traditionally constitute a graver threat. Outsiders are intruders. Always an aspect of nature, violence therefore becomes "a necessary component of life" (282). Armour, however, believes Dickey's attitude toward what happens in the wilderness is "ambiguous" (282) because he refuses to comment on the value of innocence lost and knowledge gained.

American mythology, as the title of Lewis's study indicates, sanctions all-male adventure. Novels like Melville's *Moby-Dick,* Cooper's Leatherstocking Tales, and Twain's *Adventures of Huckleberry Finn* depict fictional escapes where, as Heilbrun (1972) states, "women do not go, where civilization cannot reach, where men hunt one another like animals and hunt animals for sport" (41). *Deliverance* becomes "the apotheosis of manliness" (41) for this tradition because, having escaped the realm of women, men sexually assault one another. While Heilbrun generally centers her attack on the modern American novel, she singles out *Deliverance* as not only denying humanity to women but also devaluing feminine sensitivities and motivations that inherently exist in all individuals. Consequently, gender becomes imprisoned by an idealized male- wish fulfillment from which women need deliverance. That the novel reveals an essentially masculine vision filled with imagery of sport and violence, however, seems justifiable to Wagner (1978), for Dickey intentionally creates "a *Pilgrim's Progress* of male egoism" (49) whose aspects of physical strength, competitiveness, and sexual expectation and satisfaction all reveal an understanding and acceptance of life that goes beyond fantasy. As a story of ritual and initiation, the novel distinguishes between the expectations of the canoeists before the adventure and their recognition of certain truths after it. Each of the novel's five segments additionally possesses a unique progression which, along with the particular endings, also contributes to the book's larger unity. The "Before" section, for example, concludes with Gentry viewing the model with a "deep and complex male thrill," her golden eye "more gold than any real gold could possibly be; it was alive." Wagner believes she represents "the possibility of his returning to youth and energy" (49) because the "Before" segment centers on the dread of aging and death and the sense of inconsequence that pervades human existence. This fear of mortality drives the men to nature and an attempt to merge with its forms. The novel's circularity becomes apparent when at the conclusion of the "After" section, Gentry and Medlock settle near another lake and share their experiences, realizing now that "the *doing* is the knowledge" (50). Real control, therefore, lies not in the male bravado evidenced at the novel's opening but rather in learning to lose it.

Wagner suggests that the weakness of *Deliverance* is not the male myth but, ironically, the skillful integration of its various parts. The explicit thematic concerns apparent at the novel's beginning leave little for the reader individually to determine, and the plot, once dramatically underway, precludes excessive repetition of the theme. Dickey's rhythmic prose style, which is "incremental yet never leisurely" (52), controls through the voice of Gentry not only what is learned but the manner in which one learns it. The narrative technique involves moderately long sentences which often branch with descriptive modifiers, and shorter sentences subsequently repeat some important element from longer ones. The method owes partly to the poetic style of "On the Coosawattee," the three-part poem published first in 1962 that depicts a similar adventure, and partly to the longer narrative poems Dickey began writing in the late sixties.

In its portrayal of masculine initiation, *Deliverance* resembles "a kind of gothic, even bitter, *Adventures of Huckleberry Finn*" (Wagner 53). Rather than an idyllic passage, the journey and the primitive confrontations that occur during it require experiences and abilities not normally part of civilized life. The failure of the trip owes not to physical or moral inadequacy but to what Wagner calls "the exigencies of common sense" (53). Dickey satirizes the idea that civilization has in some sense improved men, and while he also ridicules the naive belief in simple, pastoral life, he shows that the encounter with the river effects a heightened understanding and strength in Gentry. Like Huck, he recognizes in part that any quest, without preparation or direction, is futile. Deliverance comes not from some imaginative escape from reality but from deep immersion in it. Because his malady is psychic, not physical, his salvation remains psychic, too, though caused by physical means. Carnes (1977) reiterates this view, declaring that "On the Coosawattee," without the novel's plot detail, reveals Dickey's understanding of deliverance as a "confrontation with being in all of its paradoxical aspects" (4). Only by confronting and accepting the primitive hidden within modern man and nature can one begin to live intensely.

That *Deliverance* celebrates the masculine venture, elevating the will to overcome to a heroic and even redemptive quest that becomes a passage into manhood, has not gone unchallenged. While Wagner qualifies such an interpretation, Barshay (1975), for example, asserts that the results of the river trip are "destructive, murderous, and corrosive" (169) and that the experiences suggest that the journey finally has no purpose. Bobby Trippe's rape, Lewis Medlock's broken leg, and the deaths of both mountaineers and Drew Ballinger all imply man's need for a civilized life that cultivates decency and justice. Failure to do so leads to a regression into primitive nature, symbolized by the mongoloid child with whom Drew attempts to communicate rather than by a noble savage. Strong (1978) notes that while Ed Gentry achieves re-birth, he does so only after he wounds himself; having shot his quarry, he falls from the tree where he has hidden and impales himself on his own arrow. Jungian psychology suggests that before deliverance can occur, Gentry must first re-establish contact with his primitive self, echoes of which emerge in dreams and fantasies. This union with a more basic self occurs when his two arrows simultaneously reach their targets: one strikes the mountain man and the other pierces himself, thereby establishing an awareness of the primitive man within the individual. Gentry's recognition of this connection is foreshadowed by his taking aim just where he imagines his prey to be: "We were closed together, and the feeling of a peculiar kind of intimacy increased, for he was shut within a frame within a frame, all of my making: the peep sight and the alleyway of needles, and I knew then that I had him." Strong believes the sexual suggestiveness hints that the scene consciously inverts the earlier rape scene (115). When Gentry stares into the eyes of the dead mountaineer, he thinks to himself, "You can do what you want to; nothing is too terrible. I can cut off the genitals he was going to use on me. Or I can cut off the head, looking straight into his open eyes. Or I can eat him." Having impaled himself, he then recognizes the repressed desires that acknowledge his primitive origins, an understanding achieved only through painful, physical imagery.

Taylor (1979) also disagrees that the novel celebrates male bravado, asserting that while Lewis Medlock does appeal to the masculine romantic fantasies of independence and self-assertion, his passion for the wilderness is "self-deluding posturing" (59). Rather than elevate his protagonist, Dickey reveals the river as symbolizing "the true heart of the world" (60). Kunz (1979), however, provides the most systematic rebuttal of Heilbrun, arguing that the novel does not elevate but pointedly destroys "the prison of gender"

(290). The wilderness serves as a violent initiation rite that delivers the protagonist from the captivating power of the traditional male fantasy. The two female characters, the model and Gentry's wife, have minor roles that appear peripheral to the central focus of four suburban men entering the wilderness. Yet despite their brief appearances, Dickey presents the women as "symbols of a fully realized humanity" (290) which act to free the narrator and the reader from prejudicial and stereotypical sex roles. For example, not only does Gentry confront and reject the artificial and pornographic aspects of his male-dominated profession, but later, when he visualizes the gold slice of the model's eye during intercourse with his wife, it is not because he fantasizes her as a sexual partner. Rather, the woman promises "deliverance." Avoidance of typically male behavior brings him new understanding, for when he touches her, the gold mote in her eye "fastens on" him, and Gentry thinks: "she changed completely; she looked like someone who had come to womanhood in less than a minute." Moreover, the model assists his artistic process because he brainstorms creatively later that afternoon and leaves the following day on his adventure. His wife, Martha, believes in her husband's artistic talents, though Gentry considers himself only a "mechanic of the graphic arts." Dickey associates her with two vital images, breath and spark. While he sleeps heavily, a sleep so dead that it carries him toward "a point, a line or border," Martha's breathing awakens him. Then, too, she possesses an innate spark that distinguishes her and reveals Gentry as already more free than his companions of commonplace male attitudes regarding women. He declares: "The question of beauty, beyond certain very obvious considerations, never really interested me in women; what I looked for and felt for was the spark, the absolutely personal connection, and when I found a genuine form of it, small but steady, I had married it." These images, together with Martha's vocation as a nurse, elevate her to what Kunz calls "a life-sustaining force" (293). That Gentry leaves her suggests his wife has lost some of this power, but such loss results only from Ed's perception of her and not something innate. Women in general and Martha in particular represent routine, and Gentry considers their domestic normalcy both restrictive and enervating.

While Dickey depicts the women as vital and life-sustaining, he refers to the principal male characters in terms suggesting their inadequacy (Kunz 293). Drew, Bobby, and Ed are repeatedly called "Baby," and the narrator justifies the adventure by declaring that "boys are always looking for ways to become men." The trip becomes "second-childhood game playing" (293) where the characters act out masculine roles according to the movies they have seen. Playing such games, they become less than human, "creatures" of the woods. At different times Gentry becomes like a frog, lizard, snake, dog, owl, and a "damned fucking ape." Entering nature, they really not so much flee from as toward the women because "the highway leads into the wilderness, the river toward civilization" (297). The trip, moreover, changes the men in unanticipated ways. Gentry, for instance, no longer desires to see the model's eye, which has "lost its fascination." Martha is "professional and tender, and tough, what I would have hoped for; what I knew I could have expected; what I had undervalued." Each man experiences a role reversal. While Bobby is raped, Lewis becomes dependent upon others for the first time. Ed wounds himself with his own arrow, a dramatic analogue to the earlier, threatened assault: "It was in me. *In* me. The flesh around the metal moved pitifully like a mouth, when I moved the shaft." Kunz believes that, taken together, these male characters "discover not so much how to be men as how it feels to be women abused by the kind of men they have dreamed of being" (300). *Deliverance*, therefore, exposes "the full horror of men who try to live by such a code" (301) where killing and coupling are accomplished without guilt or concern. The novel re-evaluates and alters the popular epic fantasy usually depicted in American works; previously elevated male attributes become insufficient for survival.

Winchell (1977) believes the "essentially primitivist attitude" (106) in *Deliverance* reveals three basic foci of primitivism. The cultural focus celebrates simple societies whose individuals live intimately with nature, while the psychic expresses a desire to return to childhood and to explore the hidden realm of the subconscious. Finally, the chronological views civilization in decline since some previous golden age. Overtones of all these primitivistic aspects relate to Dickey's main concern, the "heroic initiation" (106) of Gentry. Attracted to Lewis's outdoor adventurism, he manifests his vague dissatisfaction with civilized existence and yearns for the primitive with a childlike sense of escape. His interior monologues, moreover, suggest an exploration of the inner resources of the psyche (106). Because the wilderness culture and his childhood reside in the past, Gentry looks backward such that the imminent destruction of nature to create an artificial lake parallels Lewis's hope that an atomic holocaust will return mankind to savage survival. Without a nuclear war, the four canoeists return to their primeval past. However, Gentry's trip on the river, rather than a permanent escape from civilization, prepares him to live more vitally upon his return to suburbia by connecting him to his animal nature. Unlike Huck Finn, he returns "morally enhanced" (108), his initiation closely resembling the experiences in Campbell's *The Hero with a Thousand Faces*. In detailing the scenes and incidents in *Deliverance* that portray the mythic hero adventure, Winchell presents ten similar experiences from a possible sixteen described by Campbell.

That Dickey concerns himself in *Deliverance* with myth also receives attention from Jolly (1985), who suggests that the novel owes a considerable debt to Frazer's *The Golden Bough*, specifically the sections concerning sacrificial year-gods. Commenting on the ritual of sacrifice as it appears in his early poetic motion, Dickey comments in *Self-Interviews*, "A civilization had, in its early stages, a living victim who was torn apart and thrown into the nearest body of water. You can read about this in *The Golden Bough*" (90). A subtler variation of this motif appears in the novel when Drew Ballinger acts as this "living victim." Much like Orpheus, Ballinger and his music facilitate Gentry's movement from listlessness to a more vital and responsive life. His gift for playing the guitar, and therefore his affinity with Orpheus, appears early in the novel when Gentry observes, "Without having any talent, as he would be the first to tell you, Drew played mighty well, through sheer devotion." Jolly calls Ballinger's sincere interest in music a "quasi-religious dedication" (104), a devotion that brings Ballinger "Sheer joy.... Something rare and unrepeatable." Orpheus, moreover, imposed order on a chaotic world and calmed savage beasts with his lyre, an ability that resembles Ballinger's commitment, following the killing of the mountain man, to reason and authority. Though he is not dismembered before tumbling into the river, he does, like Orpheus, appear a short time later. Both become "initiates of a subliminal or spiritual world" (105) with which all men must connect in order to achieve potentiality. Gentry recognizes his debt to Ballinger when he says of the dead canoeist: "I had a friend there who in a way had died for me." Ballinger's music, his ritualistic death, and his water burial effect Gentry's ability to "regenerate himself and triumph over the 'insufficiency principle at the heart of life itself'" (107).

The inner division that afflicts Gentry and which brings about his confession of ennui and inconsequence necessitates some redemptive act. While Winchell (1977) sees a journey of the mythic hero and Jolly (1985) a sacrificial victim as responsible for Gentry's renewal, Guttenberg (1977) observes a re-integration of the divided psyche through a pattern of development that reworks the Christian myth of a fall and a subsequent redemption. The elements of this "individual apocalypse" (83) are essentially romantic because, like Wordsworth, Dickey envisions a journey both inward and outward toward wholeness. While the river becomes "a consistent symbol of the fundamental life-force" (84), another aspect of Gentry also appears, what Guttenberg calls "a Jungian shadow-self" (85), when he says to Bobby, "we'll never get out of this gorge alive" and then wonders, "Did I say that? ... Yes, a dream-man said, you did. You did say it, and you believe it." As a romantic, Dickey realizes that the wilderness represents an inner geography. The river journey, therefore, becomes analogous to Gentry's trip toward the subconscious, as when he states, "I felt the complicated urgency of the current, ... and with this came the feeling I always had at the moment of losing consciousness at night, going toward something unknown that I could not avoid, but from which I would return." His revelatory moment occurs when he discerns an inter-relationship. Beholding himself in conjunction with the water as he visualizes the river rock shaped like a face, he declares, "I can have it as I wish." Unlike Wordsworth, however, Dickey insists upon "the irredeemable savagery of the life-force" (87). The river is both "pure energy" and "unbelievable violence and brutality," a recognition that "Wordsworth's visionary moment of communion goes hand in hand with Nietzsche's Dionysian moment beyond good and evil" (88). At the top of the cliff, Gentry becomes "mindless" or pre-human, but rather than remaining in this realm, he returns to the city. Guttenberg, in language resembling Campbell's discussion of the mythic hero, asserts that his return after his spiritual communion suggests "a corresponding fall" (87). When he is catapulted from the rapids to the still water near civilization, he screams a "birth-cry" (89). His experiences repossess his divided psyche less traumatically than the Christian's fall and redemption, though Guttenberg declares that society itself continues to avoid re-integration with its shadow self by damming its rivers.

Greiner (1972) sees Dickey's central focus as less abstract than a Jungian unification of self. The violent actions and daring acrobatics reveal not only the bestiality hidden and unconfronted within all individuals but also the modern irony that survival might rely on a willing reversion to an animality once believed mastered. Purposely sketching Lewis, Bobby, and Drew as flat characters, Dickey directs reader response to his narrator and Ed's response to what he terms "harmony." His illumination means not a self-awareness of his intimate connection with Nature but "an acknowledgment of and a harmonious relationship between the two sides of his nature, the bestial and the human" (45). Preceding his adventure, he realizes that within him lies "a point, a line or border," but the movement toward recognition remains dormant until the moral dilemma concerning the body of the mountain man Lewis has killed. After the canoeists accept Lewis' plan and elevate survival over morality, Gentry states: "I got on my back and poured with the river, sliding over the stones like a creature I had always contained but never released." The simile alters *Deliverance* from an intense adventure to what Greiner posits as an investigation into the facility with which man assumes animality. The true horror of the novel, therefore, is not the homosexual rape and the killings but Dickey's implication that survival depends on a return to one's animal nature and not on conventional morality. Gentry accordingly cultivates this aspect, clinging to the cliff like a "burrowing animal," determined to be "like a creature born on the cliff and coming home." The highpoint of this identification occurs when, having wounded the second mountain man, he drops to all fours "like a dog" and tracks his prey by smelling the blood spots on the ground. The question of whether he has killed the right man, while irrelevant to his animal instincts, is crucial with regard to his humanity. His action follows another ambiguity—whether Drew was killed by a bullet. Such moral distinctions between self-defense and murder, Greiner asserts, are made meaningless in the wilderness where death simply is and animal instincts assure survival. While Gentry has previously lived by "sliding," he learns that harmony demands a balance between the bestial and the human.

Doughtie (1979), however, believes that Greiner's thesis fails to consider Dickey's emphasis on art generally and music specifically. Dickey shows art to be "a necessary mediator between nature—both the exterior nature of woods and the interior nature of man's drives and dreams—and modern urban 'civilized' life" (167). Both realms possess their virtues and horrors, and while art is a product of civilization, it also remains connected with the primitive. For Dickey, moreover, genuine art "embraces both Dionysis and Apollo" (168). Gentry's discontent with civilization derives from the false art around him. His advertising studio restricts aspiration and achievement such that he depreciates his artistic abilities. His gradual embrace of primitive or Dionysian forces is assisted by art, which provides him models and also channels these natural forces through reference to the movies. When, for example, Lewis breaks his leg coming over the falls, Gentry remarks that "the cliff looked like a gigantic drive-in movie screen waiting for an epic film to begin." Assessing their predicament, he later states they will "never get out of this gorge alive" because the mountaineer "means to pick the rest of us off tomorrow." The words sound theatrical, and Gentry asks, "When do the movies start, Lord?" Doughtie suggests that movies, because of their remoteness from real experience, provide role models for behavior, and Gentry assumes that of the Western gunslinger (172). Movies also become "a metaphor for the act of the imagination" (173). Climbing the cliff, he imagines reaching the top: "I could get there in my mind. The whole thing focused, like an old movie that just barely held its own on the screen." Doughtie calls this "Ed's own mental movie" (173) and believes it the beginning of the empathetic imagination needed to confront his enemy. Later, Gentry responds to the river's visual beauty and also to his imaginative vision: "*What* a view. But I had my eyes closed. The river was running in my mind, and I raised my lids and saw exactly what had been the image of my thoughts." The return to civilization requires further use of art, specifically that of realistic fiction, as Gentry creates the story needed to satisfy the police. He says to Bobby, "Control, baby. It can be controlled," and talking to the authorities, he thinks: "I made it a point to try to visualize the things I was saying as though they really happened.... for me they were happening as I talked." Art becomes, finally, "the true control of nature and reality" (175) and *Deliverance* "a kind of extended metaphor for the poetic process" (179). In imposing order on chaos, the artist most clearly discerns the elements of disorder. Consequently, Gentry must understand the true nature of his situation, believe in his actions, and choose.

Anderson (1986) also believes that Gentry's role as artist provides the foundation for the novel. Despite Connell's (1976) objection, first-person narration is uniquely appropriate because "the *real* story" (12) evolves within Gentry's consciousness, a perspective that lends itself to the "psychic and spiritual dislocation" (12) revealed by his attitudes toward George Holley's obsession with art and with Braque's collage technique. His re-telling shows the reconciliation of his past knowledge with his present understanding, an aesthetic re-integration best provided by Gentry's own ordering of details and events into a novel. He gives form to experience and in so doing remembers past action and dialogue. As his artistic abilities become enhanced, so too are the images, which display depth, color, and texture. His narrative consequently seeks harmony in presenting its relationships so that art then becomes his deliverance (15).

Beidler's (1972) analysis detects Dickey's concern with art but reaches a different conclusion. Gentry shoots an innocent hunter rather than the second mountain man, and he recognizes this fact: "I believe that if I could have seen him move I would have known, one way or the other. But I didn't, and I don't." Consequently, he endeavors to escape from his guilt because, although he can justify killing a perverted rapist, he cannot conceive himself murdering an innocent man. Dickey's "supreme accomplishment" (33) is that he crafts his narrator as a man who believes his actions to be just and who, when confronted with the face of a man he has intended to kill, also suppresses his error by becoming caught up in his own fiction. Gentry dislikes discord: "I liked harmoniousness and a situation where the elements didn't fight with each other or overwhelm eath other." On the cliff he imposes a harmony on the potentially conflicting elements ("For a second I did not know what I was seeing and what I was imagining; there was such an utter sameness that it didn't matter.") Returning to civilization, he rehearses his story, which "had become so strong in my mind that I had trouble getting back through to the truth," a difficulty enhanced by his tendency to confuse real life with the movies. Beidler believes Dickey's narrator possesses "an unusually highly developed capacity for imposing his own patterns on reality" (35) and that the novel's epigraph implies that Gentry's pride finally undoes him. His artistic abilities, therefore, become only a means of self-deception. Proud of assuming the hero's role, he is then unable to conceive of himself as a villain.

Other critics see *Deliverance* not so much as presenting art as *a* thematic concern but as *the* central subject of the novel. Markos (1971), for instance, believes the novel appraises the importance of immediacy in human life and appears to be "a veiled statement about the awakening of the artist through the experience of beauty and terror" (950). While *Deliverance* does glorify manhood as epitomized by physical fitness, bravery, and resourcefulness, it implicitly celebrates art. Likening it to Whitman's "Out of the Cradle" and Wordsworth's *The Prelude*, Markos states that nature mysticism effects Gentry's artistic awakening; by confronting extreme danger, he achieves "the necessary freshening of perceptions" (951). Both Medlock and Gentry also possess a fantasy life that delivers them from ennui. Regardless of what the fantasy involves, its presence gives these characters an identity, and although only the narrator subsequently attains a sense of the transcendent, he mentally holds it like a possession. Medlock finds himself becoming a Zen archer, having partly lived his fantasy; and while Gentry's own fantasy involving the model has also lost its power, his experiences have partly energized him, though "his rebirth is incomplete" (953). The novel's ending, then, suggests that such vivid experience lives only "in memory or art" (952).

While Markos suggests that *Deliverance* indirectly offers a study of artistic imagination and its efforts to invent or compose consequence, Lindborg (1974) argues that the novel presents it directly. Though the work belongs to a tradition that, beginning with James Fenimore Cooper, involves the hunt and killing, Dickey's focus is "an exploration of the process of creation" (84). While nature provides Gentry with his final understanding of art, he possesses creativity even in the city, though it is mainly mechanical and never brings him into an intimate connection with his subject. However, once making a decision to canoe the river, he feels even in his office "a powerful sense of being in a place he had created." The book depicts his subsequent efforts to project his conceptions into reality. Compelled by images of himself as a hunter and explorer, he uses fantasy to make reality, thinking: "I liked the idea, and the image, I must say. I touched the knife hilt at my side, and remembered that all men were once boys, and that boys are always looking for ways to become men." Stalking a deer, he discovers that "hunting and pretending to hunt had come together." In acting out a role, Gentry becomes the persona. His climb up the cliff becomes "the culmination of this vision" (88) because he projects "the human into nature; man is a god—it is the eye which creates" (88). Consequently, the river assumes the face of a god, and the mountain man, when Gentry sees him at dawn, possesses "the most beautiful or convincing element of design." Connecting with a power beyond himself, he recognizes that "nothing is too terrible," and though he resists savagery, he understands that the force at life's center is indifferent, occasionally requiring a blood sacrifice that mandates a personal response. The novel itself then is "a means of discovery" (90). Rather than lighting out for the territory like Huck, slowly retreating from civilization like Natty Bumppo, or living in lonely sainthood like Ike McCaslin, the individual must "tap the vital force of nature through art" (90). In re-telling his adventure, Gentry does just that.

Discussions about the American Adam in a new Eden, the noble savage and civilization, and amoral violence all miss what Davis (1976) considers the novel's multiple ironies. Critics like Armour (1978) believe the canoeists must enter the wilderness without the weapons of civilization, and Cavell (1971), for example, agrees, declaring, "Loyal to the rules of their game, they leave technology behind and take only bows and arrows" (117). Yet Gentry's description of his bow and arrows clearly reveals their technological advancements. Wearing a nylon suit, carrying a "hardware store knife," and riding in a canoe of "factory metal" all underscore modern man's dependency on technology. Dickey also treats his characters ironically. Bobby Trippe, the man most acclimated to soft city life, suffers the least amount of injury while doing the least to assist in the adventure. He even fails the one important task assigned him by Gentry, who angrily yells: "You didn't start on time, you did everything worng. I ought to take this rifle and shoot the hell out of you, Bobby, you incompetent asshole, you soft city country-club man." Ed himself recognizes the irony inherent in their conversation: "You'd have been dead, you should've been dead, right about exactly now." Drew Ballinger, by contrast, seems attuned to nature, his "inherent rapport" (Davis 225) most evident when he plays the guitar. In his unthinking, spontaneous responses, he even resembles what Ed calls the "mindlessness" of the wilderness. Yet he is the only one among the city men to die. Moreover, while Lewis talks about elemental survival, he remains urbanized. Gentry recognizes that he remains too indoctrinated by the city to escape: "He talked continuously of resettling in New Zealand or South Africa or Uruguay, but he had to be near the rental property he had inherited, and I didn't much think he would ever leave." Despite his physical fitness, Lewis becomes the most dependent on others. Gentry, the most changed by the drama, remains undecided as to the adventure's value, for he does not consider his transformation completely favorable. He says of the ambulance driver who carries him to the hospital, "He not only felt good to me, but he felt like a good person, and I needed one bad." Gentry's transformation ironically depends upon the fabrication of what happened on the river, a lie that highlights a major theme in *Deliverance*—the line between reality and truth on the one hand and appearance and deception on the other remains problematic (228). So strongly does Gentry assimilate his created version that he has difficulty distinguishing it from what actually occurred. Dickey implies, therefore, that while the individual may attempt a spiritual cleansing through nature, the effort will not bring re-birth. He will instead realize that truth has many versions and that social institutions like marriage and the law remain necessary for men to survive in a technological century.

Schmitt (1991) believes that the "ironic components" (9) of *Deliverance* reveal Dickey's questioning of the modern applicability of man's affinity to nature. Rather than enhancing the male fantasy of a noble return to primitivism, the irony inverts it as another aspect of Dickey's belief in "the creative possibilities of the lie" (*Self-Interviews* 32). The novel creates "an unresolved and unresolvable tension" (10) between the hero's quest for the enlightened initiation of the wilderness and modern man's state of irreversible and technological alienation from nature. Dickey subverts the stereotypical views that nature is submissive and feminine, that primitive savages are noble and moral, and that the fittest survive, reversals that thrust the reader into "the wilderness of moral relativity" (10). Schmitt also argues that while Dickey acknowledges the influence of Campbell's *The Hero with a Thousand Faces*, his characterizations of the four canoeists are "ironic modern manifestations" (10) of Campbell's transformations of the hero as warrior, lover, emperor/tyrant, and redeemer/saint. Lewis, the hero as warrior, becomes powerless against not only the river but also the forces of civilization that necessitate the adventure. Bobby, the most "feminine" of the men, ironically reverses the hero as lover by having to care for Lewis after being rescued himself following his violation. As the ironic modern example of the hero as emperor/tyrant, Gentry achieves a communion with the natural world and yet shows "a negative movement toward tyranny" (14) in his subsequent attitudes toward Bobby and the mountain man he has killed. Finally, Drew exhibits Dickey's ironic portrayal of the hero as redeemer/saint, a depiction revealed in his wife's reaction to his death. She says to Gentry, "It's all so useless," and her comment reinforces the point that nothing good comes of his death since its circumstances remain a secret. These ironic reversals of Campbell's hero suggest Dickey's belief that "We must write new myths" (15) because past definitions of heroism no longer suffice. Not only does the status as archetypal hero become impossible but so does cultural initiation. Mythic identity quests in the technological world no longer follow the pattern of development prescribed by the ancient monomyth, which stresses skills concerning the intimate comprehension of nature.

Given the mediocrity of urban life and the gulf separating man from his origins, the search for consequence assumes larger proportions, an odyssey in which the hero must recover what he has lost. In his analysis of the novel's development as a genre, Adams (1973) asserts that *Deliverance* depicts the epic tradition in at least three primary ways. First, the book "speaks for a sedentary generation" (309), one which longs to escape the constraints of civilized life and return to the primitive outdoors. Second, the narrator unwillingly assumes the role of hero when confronted by adversity and saves both himself and two of his friends. Finally, *Deliverance* offers a "veiled allegory with an obvious moral" (309). The canoeists leave the modern city and descend into a canyon to find "their river and their epic hell" (309). When Gentry ascends the cliff and kills his adversary, he rises literally and figuratively. Paradoxically, a civilized man armed with a primitive weapon kills a primitive man with an advanced weapon, such that Gentry momentarily becomes "Odysseus putting out the eyes of Polyphemus" (309). Dickey completes the allegory by having the river, which is both beautiful and savage, rise to cover and obliterate the voyage to Hades.

Scholars who attempt to determine the genre to which *Deliverance* properly belongs have also initiated a more specific analysis of narrative strategy. Marin (1970), for instance, argues that Dickey primarily strives to capture reader believability with language that demands attention. Gentry's voice focuses and compels in the tensity of his diction, the blend toward fantasy, and the startling clarity of perception (51), all of which serve as a camera to concentrate description into "a foreshortened compactness more powerfully convincing than anything the naked eye feels" (51). However, because the novel is one of place and act rather than character, Dickey stresses scenes by insisting on extensive detail and immediate sensory experience and avoiding summation except in the "Before" and "After" sections. Characterization is accomplished "deftly with straight, heavy strokes" (52). Gentry is the most rounded; the others are aspects of his personality, a technique that maintains "sharp narrative focus" (54) since Dickey intends to depict how the river and surrounding wilderness affect Ed. Marin sees his journey as a trek into a repressed human consciousness, comparing the journey to Marlow in Conrad's *Heart of Darkness* and Brown in Hawthorne's "Young Goodman Brown." Moreover, Dickey juxtaposes images throughout the novel in order to articulate his "structure of meaning" (56). The cat's claws stuck in the model's panties parallel the owl's talons puncturing the tent top, and Gentry's imagined hunt with the owl soon gives way to stalking first a deer and then another man. Only the discussion between Lewis and Ed as they drive into the country of the hill people, talk which lasts about fifteen pages, loosens and weakens Dickey's rhetorical strategy since it slows the narrative pace.

Holley (1978) declares that Gentry's vivid sense of design reveals the novel's structure and that imagination, not simply physical fitness or animal instinct, provides a deliverance that is also the book's climax. Gentry seeks out harmony, concentrating on the physical detail that frames into proper perspective the thing observed, whether it be an attractive model, an owl or deer, a river, a cliff, or a human target. His "focusing imagination" (91) brings him ever deeper into his subject and parallels the novel's movement, a relationship evidenced by changes in his state of sleep in the three sections within the frame of *Deliverance*. Early in the narrative, Gentry's lethargy and tendency toward heavy sleep result only in weary inexactness, but his climb up the cliff figuratively awakens him from death as he newly sees the river: "But it was not seeing, really. For once it was not just seeing. It was beholding." When his victim appears at dawn, Gentry frames him with pine needles and then with the string sight of his bow. From noting the gold slice in the model's eye to the interim scenes involving the second mountain man, he achieves his clarity in stages. When he sights his prey, thinking "I had never seen a more beautiful or convincing element of design," he finally arrives at his deepest understanding because now "both physical and mental energies are brought into the organizing influence of the frame" (97). The imagination discovers a focus and design shaping the separate details, and Gentry's arrow finds its mark. Similarly, Dickey brackets his adventure with the "Before" and "After" sections to establish "the structural and thematic patterns of the novel" (93), thereby eliminating extraneous detail like Gentry's office routine. The sectional frames move the reader deeper into the narrative until one sees Gentry achieve creative focus. Form and matter, Holley argues, achieve relationship, and Dickey's protagonist is delivered from death in the climactic scene.

In addition to analyzing structure and design, critics apply Marxist as well as psychological interpretations. For example, while Jameson (1972) admits the canoeists' victory over their adversaries and their return from nature constitutes an initiation ritual, he believes Dickey's choice of subject matter reveals "the necessity of violence, both on the individual and the social level" (182). Though an intimate part of life, violence has become mitigated by civilized life, but *Deliverance* admits "a kind of ideological double standard" (182) by allowing the reader to experience vicariously the human instinct for violence while simultaneously positing the need for authority on a social and political level. Jameson asserts that the adventure apparently results from a "basic dissatisfaction with the structure of middle-class life" (182), but Medlock's fear that "the machines are going to fail, the political systems are going to fail" hides a deeper social and political concern about monopolistic capitalism and its computerized industries. It confirms the modern anxiety of some fundamental schism between individual life and the social structure. The canoeists' physical efforts in the wilderness constitute "counter-insurgency warfare, a way of beating the enemy at his own game" (185). The perversion and violence are therefore appropriate because the heroes struggle against a class of people who consider themselves equal and who rise up against them, a situation which accounts for the indignation of the suburbanites. However, Dickey's treatment of the social terror bothers Jameson, who believes the novelist lacks acute awareness of this horror, as do his characters. *Deliverance* becomes then "not an instrument of ideological demystification, but rather an outright political and social wish-fulfill-ment" (186), merely reinforcing engrained attitudes whose purgation remains the genuine function of art.

Schechter's (1980) psychological study attempts to determine the literary value of *Deliverance* by showing its relationship to a work already estab-lished in the canon. Noting that critics fault the novel for its male bravado, its two-dimensional characterization, and an artistic slickness that conceals pat literary formulas and contrivances, he nevertheless admits to its pervasive and compelling power. This effect owes to "the richness of its mythic or archetypal imagery" (7), which reaches into the unconscious through primordial images while the narrative, seemingly lacking in psychological portrayal, presents a nightmarish world. The story follows the archetypal pattern of the hero's quest, the departure from the common world after receiving a call to adventure and the crossing of a threshold into a region of dangerous and heightened powers. Having undergone a series of initiating tasks, the hero returns transfigured and rewarded with spiritual illumination. Schechter, however, discerns an underlying psychological meaning in the myth, a Jungian perspective suggested by the book's two epigraphs. The first, by George Bataille, translates, "There exists at the base of human life an element of incompleteness," and describes the protagonist's problem. The second, from Obadiah, provides a solution: "The pride of thine heart hath deceived them, thou that dwellest in the clefts of the rock, whose habitation is high; that saith in his heart, Who shall bring me down to the ground?" Gentry's malaise is nowhere better presented than when he thinks, "The feeling of the inconsequence of whatever I would do, of anything I would pick up or think about or turn to see was at that moment being set in the very bone marrow. How does one get through this? I asked myself." Social adaption, which has stultified his psychological development by repressing his natural instincts, requires him to abandon both his middle-class city complacency and middle-aged sense of futility. He must leave the "gentry" to be "brought down to the ground." Interpreted psychologically, such an injunction refers not to the back-to-nature narrative but to "a *successful* hunt for selfhood, a hero's quest which culminates in a genuine rebirth" (10).

Schechter argues that individuation, which most often appears as a fervent desire to undertake a journey, links *Deliverance* and *Moby-Dick*. Like Ahab, Lewis, suffering a neurotic fear of death and described as "obsessed" and "fanatical," compels the other men into the trip. Drew Ballinger, steadfast and domestic, resembles Starbuck; both are incapacitated by normalcy. On the other hand, Bobby Trippe parallels Stubb, Melville's friendly but shallow clown, who journeys into the vast unknown without ever comprehending the experience. Like Ismael, who along with the rest of the ship's crew succumbs to Ahab's rhetoric, Ed Gentry becomes caught up in his friend's talk until he feels "his capricious and tenacious enthusiasm." The difference is that Medlock sees the wilderness as a personal testing ground for his physical prowess, while Ed observes the map of the area from the "standpoint of design." Despite the meandering colors, he notes "harmony of some kind."

Gentry feels compelled to travel into the wilderness, believing it promises spiritual wholeness. As he journeys deeper into the North Georgia woods, he contacts "the alien forces of the psyche" (12) in those scenes depicting his entrance into the river and his dreamlike experience with the owl, a creature of night vision and wisdom whose contact with the hero constitutes "the breakdown of the barrier between the ego and the unconsciousness" (13). Self-realization begins with the recognition of the shadow archetype, who embodies bestial qualities and who represents the repressed aspect of one's personality. This process of acknowledging the hidden, primitive instincts starts when the first mountaineer is killed and Gentry becomes an accomplice to Lewis's plan to bury the corpse, but is not completed until he fully assimilates his shadow self. After climbing the mountain and penetrating "the tomb-womb of the Great Mother" (14), an act of incestuous renewal, Gentry confronts the personification of his brutal animality in the second mountaineer. Dickey depicts a strange intimacy between them, and with the mountaineer's death, Gentry achieves his shadow, having acknowledged its existence shortly beforehand by tracking his wounded victim "like a dog." When the rope lowering them both down the cliff snaps and the hero plunges into the river, he experiences his ritual death. The icy water finally prepares him for deliverance, his reintegration into the civilized world completing "the mythic pattern which structures his story: separtion-initiation-return" (16-17). Gentry, in effect, has become a new being; his possession of imaginative powers at the novel's conclusion reveals the connection with the psyche's creativity.

Recognition of a dark personality within the individual, particularly as it relates both to the hero's search and the nature of deliverance, leads critics like Longen (1977) and Italia (1975) to examine Dickey's presentation of sex, lust, and love. Longen contends that once ethics have been discarded and courtesy and convention eliminated, what remains is life made "meaningful and operative primarily in physical, sexual terms" (137). Sex initiates Gentry's weekend adventure when he and his wife make love in a position purposely designed to contrast with the later homosexual rape. During intercourse, Gentry sees the model's gold eye in the middle of Martha's back. It shines "not with the practicality of sex, so necessary to its survival, but the promise of it that promised other things, another life, deliverance." His use of the word "deliverance," its only occasion in the novel, suggests his belief that sex remains one of the few moments in civilized life when the individual fully experiences his body and spirit; its intimacy and physicality enable him to "feel himself alive all the way" (139). That the sex is heterosexual and caring and that it occurs with his wife in their bedroom in the city constitute behavioral norms for Gentry. By contrast, the homosexual rape of Bobby is ugly and brutal, undertaken with an utter disregard that also characterizes the attitude of nature as the suburban canoeists struggle downstream. Gentry's recognition that nature's actions are essentially physical and indifferent and that his response must be similar primarily accounts for his success in saving the others. His climb up the cliff wall becomes sexual, his motion slow, insistant, and intimate until he reaches the top and thinks: "I was crawling, but it was no longer necessary to make the cliff, to fuck it for an extra inch or two in the moonlight...." Moreover, his killing of the mountaineer is "orgasmic" (145) because Gentry passes out after first becoming excited, confused, and breathless and then experiencing a literal sense of falling. His survival, then, is sexual. He recognizes that merely changing one's place or activity will not renew an individual and that the deliverance earlier promised by only physical sex is an illusion. Sex, in fact, connects one to darker forces. Longen believes that for Dickey sex is "precisely the possibility, even if rarely realized, of the surrender of reason to a power and a feeling that completely overwhelm it, even if only for a moment" (148). This potential is the nature of deliverance in sex, and it also reflects the sexual nature in Ed's killing of the mountain man, having released within himself "an underground river of great depth and power" (149).

Italia observes the "macabre symmetry" (204) of having an anal sodomist die from an arrow through the back and a potential oral sodomist from an arrow in the throat. However, such poetic justice masks a deeper "mystery" (204) formed between a civilized and a primitive hunter and where love results from death. The attack by the mountain men establishes "the pattern of the book: struggle, copulation, and death" (204), but Italia argues that Gentry's retaliatory pursuit is essentially sexual and parallels his earlier pursuit of his wife. Not only does she assume a physical position of sodomy, but Gentry's imaginative vision of the nearly naked model "threaten[s] to turn the love-act into a rape" (209). Just as the climax of the love scene, moreover, results in the novel's title, so does the hunt scene, the book's climax, provide its meaning. Dickey subtly reveals love emerging from perversity. Gentry feels "a peculiar kind of intimacy" for the mountaineer and admits, "There was something relaxed and enjoying in his body position." The hunt ends with both men feeling a sudden blast and falling as they perform "a macabre parody of sexual union" (207), and Gentry subsequently discovers himself "giving birth to his own freedom" (210). Having killed the primitive side of himself by paradoxically becoming primitive, he becomes more civilized and reveals his new-found love by taking the model to dinner, re-hiring a former employee, and accepting his own artistic abilities. Love and death are therefore inextricably united, and sex becomes "the energy that shapes all life" (212). It appears in the business world and the wilderness and not simply the bedroom, having only little to do with normal or abnormal physical coupling.

Monk (1977) examines the novel's color symbolism, which Dickey links to his hero's evolution in attitude. Gentry attributes the awakening of his sensibilities to learning how to kill a man after first overcoming any misgivings. His consciousness further develops not only when he recognizes the occasional need for violence but also when he feels "its terrible beauty" (262). However, using his eyes, he continually locates himself according to how and what he sees. His office world is drab and colorless, the studio full of "grey affable men" with "grey and bald heads in their places." He hardly recognizes the nearness of autumnal color, but responding to the model's appearance, a slice of her eye that is "more gold than any real gold could possibly be," he immediately feels hit by "strong powers." Three subsequent experiences effect his rejection of man-made color and light: his reaction against modern architecture while driving into the wilderness; the episode at Griner Brothers' Garage, a half-rustic, half-industrial world where the glowing "luminous and green" batteries suggest debasement; and the scene in which the canoeists commit themselves to the river at a place where the blues and greens of nature have become perverted by the litter and pollution of civilization (264-65). When Gentry more fully enters the wilderness, these natural colors reassert themselves. However, they also constitute "a kind of trickery in the landscape" (266) for they deceptively hide the river's dangerous depths and contours. The canoeists' "hubristic reliance on the man-made" (266), apparent at the book's opening when they examine the map's colors, causes their failure to perceive perspective correctly. Even their equipment, almost all of it "different shades of green," reflects their lack of fitness. Gentry, already suspicious of light and color because of his profession, learns "to find himself at the center of his senses, perhaps *beyond* them" (268). Monk argues that as a result of his experiences, "we feel Gentry *discovering* significance through sight, and the limitations of sight" (278). Dickey does not impose a color scheme. Rather, transcendence lies in "the autonomous context of the action" (278). Gentry does not learn a schematic use of color—blacks and whites for civilization, blues and greens that treacherously reverse themselves in nature, and gold for femininity. Instead, he comprehends how color works as a principle.

Edwards's (1973) critical study of the novel's eye and owl imagery further develops Dickey's anti-romantic view of primitive man. Owl images occur in three specific places: the paragraph description of the artificial owl on Gentry's porch, the live owl that hunts from the top of Gentry's tent, and Gentry's identification with that owl when its talons grip his finger. As nocturnal birds of prey that symbolize both ill-omen and wisdom, the owl enhances the narrative, but by having the living owl replace the "wind-toy," Dickey contrasts the harmless with the real when the suburbanites enter the woods. Because Gentry thinks again of the artificial bird after his return to civilization, the progression of owl images over three days "retraces the course of human development" (97)—the men shed their civilized habits, become savage and violent, and then cover up the horror by assuming their casual activities. Dickey links the owl's meaning with significant eye imagery. The chicken head, with its "glazed eye half-open, looking right at me and through me," and Gentry's own eyes that night, "looking up through almost closed lids," both suggest a "mechanical working" where the vision of reality remains incomplete (98). The chicken's stare resembles that of the owl, which represents the new knowledge to which Gentry must come. With its gold slice, the model's eye parallels the half-open eyes of the owl. The conventional connotations of gold as valuable and the owl as vicious suggest that "viciousness is basic to human nature" (99). The model's eye appears four times in the novel, the first three all connected with sexual arousal. After his adventure, however, when Gentry takes her to dinner, "her gold-halved eye had lost its fascination. Its place was in the night river, in the land of impossibility." Dickey therefore implies that sex remains civilized man's lone connection to the primitive instincts mandatory in his natural state.

Appearing seventeen years after *Deliverance*, *Alnilam* (1987), a massive novel of 682 pages, received mixed reviews. Expecting a work similar to *Deliverance*, critics were baffled by its lack of action and slow pacing and by a stylistic innovation whereby particular pages were split into parallel columns to suggest the visible world as it is ordinarily perceived and as Frank Cahill, the blind protagonist, mentally envisions it. Reviewers also cited weak characterization and a poetic prose that occasionally yields to overwriting, flaws similarly mentioned regarding Dickey's first novel. While he was teaching at Rice Institute in 1952, Dickey originally conceived the plot of a father who has lost his son early in World War II in a training accident. The narrative, portions of which were first published in *Esquire* in February 1976, developed only slowly. Because of the novel's length and its many layers of meaning, reviewers variously identified its principal theme. Dickey, however, commenting during the book's composition, declared his intent directly: "The main thing I want to do with *Alnilam*, is to write the ultimate novel of fathers and sons; the mysteries, the frustrations, the revelations, and, in the end, the eventual renunciation and reconciliation" (Bruccoli 14). Along with this he planned to show both "the dangerous-ness—the sheer *dangerousness*—of ideas. Their applicability can result in the deaths and mutilations of many" and what he labels "the concept of the *fabulous* death" (11-12). He recognized that both *Alnilam* and its intended sequel *Crux* endeavor to treat so many ideas that their full development and integration remain questionable. While his thematic concerns involve personal, military, artistic, and social relationships, as well as their implications, he states, "I think the crux of the matter lies somewhere in the definition of what power does to a man, and also charlatanry, and also love" (15). Taken together, he intends the two novels to "open out from a small incident at a primary training base into a vast Tolstoyan vision of the Pacific night air war" (15).

Parini (1987) thinks the novel disappointing, calling it a "melodrama" that is "windy, often incoherently organized, and—sometimes—downright bad" (70), particularly when Dickey splits the narrative into vertical columns to reflect in dark bold type Frank Cahill's subjective impressions. Though a father's search for his son has old literary antecedents, the experimental technique makes Dickey seem "desperate to strike a post-modern note" (70). Stating that the "split-screen device" renders *Alnilam* "mechanically, as well as conceptually, hard to read" (25), the unnamed reviewer in *Playboy*, which featured an interview with Dickey in November 1973, labels the work "long and windy" and hopes that "Dickey has gotten this one out of his system"

(25). Towers (1987) praises the novel's set pieces: the dog fight where Zack, Cahill's enormous animal guide, kills an entire pack of local dogs and the scenes where Hannah, a young woman who knew Joel, Cahill's son, cares for his father's needs. However, while the novel is ambitious and overreaching, it is alternately pretentious and hindered by windiness and slow pacing. The scrutiny required for the split columns of prose often brings some startling or original play of language, but when the narrative moves "like lava oozing from a fissure" in a work "Melvillean in its aspirations and scope" (7), these sections seem merely digressive. Dickey never renders clearly enough the mystery of Alnilam, the secret group Joel has created and which plans to take over the military, and its demonstration of power, designed to be the book's climax, remains weak. The novel lacks what Towers calls "a white whale to pursue" (7).

Steinberg (1987) also notes the slight narrative line for so large a fictional work and believes its size is "clearly only an excuse for Dickey to work out a series of often profound, sometimes merely glib ruminations" (65). The unnamed reviewer sees Dickey's subjects as the mystery of flight, the nature of war, male bonding, and the mystical quality of leadership. Providing the focus for these concerns is the "starkly contrasting worlds of vision and blindness" (65), the principal lens by which Dickey views them. Taylor (1987) more specifically considers the theme that of literal, imaginative, and transcendental flight, all of which reflect the human need "of determining precise positions" (15). Kerley (1987) asserts that *Alnilam* becomes "essentially a labyrinth of questions about identity" (55), while Medwick (1987) views it as "a book about male potency: the depths from which it erupts ("alnilam" writ "animal"?) and the heights to which it soars" (118). Chappell (1987) believes its final intent is "a warning against mystic charisma" (6F). Baughman (1987) discerns the many forms of power that radiate from and act on the individual and declares that *Alnilam* shows the need to rise above inconsequence. The danger of attaining that "intensified life" is its lack of control, such that "its practitioner can become a monomaniac like Captain Ahab in *Moby-Dick* or Lewis Medlock in *Deliverance*" (S1). Only Starr (1987) identifies the theme of father and son relationships which Dickey himself states as his primary intent.

Without scrutinizing narrative motive, critics generally condemn Dickey's characterization. Steinberg (1987) dismisses it as "seldom very convincing" except for Colonel Hoccleve, the base commander, though the dialogue is "a haunting blend of eloquence and rough country speech" (65). Chappell (1987) believes only Cahill and his dog are convincing, complaining that all the characters talk "as if they had fallen into a vat of Thomas Wolfe prose and had swallowed more than they could ingest" (6F). Apologetic, Taylor (1987) observes that *Alnilam* unites two vastly different tendencies in Southern literature: an appreciation for common speech and ordinary characters and the inclination to employ new fictional techniques. If Dickey's characters think more deeply and speak more eloquently than seem likely, then the reader should remember that the author is a poet writing about the nature of stars and men as well as their relationship. Towers (1987), however, states that Dickey's sense of local dialect and mannerisms is "impeccable" and declares that only Joel remains enigmatic, a trait deliberately intended. Joel is partly a Shelleyan idealist, partly a dangerous monster of ego, and partly a prophet who voices empty oracles. He advocates what he terms "precision mysticism," using gnomic aphorisms to advance his Zen-like belief in the extension of man and airplane that, in turn, leads to an intimacy between the individual and the element of air. Before his death, he attracts a following of men who contend that his system of coded numbers yields balance and universal position. He plans to extend his revolutionary movement, named Alnilam after the middle star in the belt of Orion the Hunter, to other air bases. Eventually Joel wants to change human consciousness, using the star he calls "the moving center." Taylor (1987) and Kerley (1987) additionally note that Cahill and his wolf-dog are earthly incarnations of Orion and his dog, Sirius.

Chappell (1987) believes that the novel's structure is so exhaustively prepared and intricately built that its success depends upon a single scene, the disruption of the air cadet graduation ceremonies, which Dickey "shirked" (6F). *Alnilam* is fundamentally a mystery story, and while having a large, unresolved question at its heart is apropos, the failure of the climactic scene renders the mystery only murk (6F). Baughman (1987) implies that the structure relates not so much to narrative events as to the development of Frank Cahill. He is "a kind of Oedipus, a blind man seeking and discovering many truths" (S8). Isolated from life, he creates a private, artificial world, an amusement park for swimmers and bodybuilders, that becomes "his personal Garden of Eden" (S1). He then confronts Alnilam, "the apparent emblem of the intensified life" (S8). Bonded in male camaraderie, its members share a youthful arrogance against authority and believe that man can transcend his limitations. Although Cahill loses his physical vision, he learns to develop the heightened responses of other senses, not only those of smell, taste, touch, and sound but also of memory, dreams, and imagination. Because of his experiences, he achieves "a kind of inner sight" (Baughman S8).

Critical studies of *Alnilam* presently focus on the mythological and philosophical subtexts. Kerley ("Understanding" 1987) asserts that the myth of Orion centers the novel's "structure, its metaphoric mysteries, and its motifs of sight and blindness" (15) because Dickey has personalized the Orion story. Since he fears, as he writes in his essay "The Imagination as Glory," "the silence of the infinite spaces" (Weigl and Hummer 166), he attempts in *Alnilam* to answer the question of the constellation's meaning. His interest has evidenced itself throughout his career in such poems as "For the Nightly Ascent of the Hunter Orion over a Forest Clearing" (1962) and *The Zodiac* (1976). That Orion occupies a central position in the winter sky, that he was once blind and then restored to sight, and that he was initially earthbound and subsequently placed in the heavens are all aspects of the myth Dickey incorporates in the novel. Frank Cahill undergoes the rites of passage of the archetypal hero. Called to action by the notification of Joel's death, despite his never having seen his son, Cahill simultaneously becomes separated from the world by his blindness. The novel's action resides in his finding his lost son and in the process himself. Though a return to sight remains impossible, Cahill "*sees* in colors, illumination, and insight" (18). While *Alnilam* reveals the story of that journey, the book's ultimate goal is "to balance the myth of Orion against Frank's own story" (19). Like the star Alnilam, Joel holds the conspiracy together; he is the center, and while he remains distant, his designs need explication. His father, who talks constantly about balance, similarly holds the novel together as he attempts to understand the myth his son has become.

Kerley (1989) believes *Alnilam* exhibits the same detail, insistence on spiritual survival, and lyrical impulse as Dickey's poetry (18). It also shares with *Deliverance* the identical romantic sensibility that creates the poems, and he catalogues the similarities between the two novels. For example, both involve hunters and both stress an essentially lyric quality of the romantic vision, including the idea of transcendence, the use of imagination to comprehend and create, the belief that personality acts as an indicator of change, and the use of language to confront and change reality. In addition, *Deliverance* and *Alnilam* utilize mythology to reinforce the hero's quest. Each concerns a man who is either figuratively or literally blind and whose "deliverance" derives from a dangerous adventure as the protagonist comes to understand brotherhood on different levels (19). Brewer (1990) also discerns similarity in the novels and traces the hero's mythic journey in each book. Admitting that the three days of the canoe trip in *Deliverance* more clearly delineate the protagonist's separation, penetration, and return, she argues that Cahill's initiation into the larger realm of air, having first left his amusement park and entered a world of blindness, is marked by several tests that evaluate his intuition. The ride in a Link Trainer and his piloting a Stearman enable Cahill to connect with "an element of power, in this instance, air" (12-13). His nearness to death ironically brings him closer to life, and he returns to his former surroundings not only able to identify with people but even seeking them. Stating that air is "the true protagonist" (12) in the novel, Dickey declares:

> Frank Cahill is different at the end of *Alnilam*; not greatly differ-ent—he still has his iron will and his truculence—but changed in some essential ways. This is partly shown by the fact that he does not plan to get another dog.... It is also signified by the fact that he wants to take Hannah with him, and establish some kind of life with her, though they are both seriously impaired.... He is a little more humanized, and less fanatical, and because of this he may possibly come to understand his enigmatic son in ways not possible before. (Brewer 13-14)

Cahill, like Gentry, becomes transformed into what Brewer calls "a force as mysterious as the force made in his connection" (14).

Covel (1989) examines the philosophical subtext that informs *Alnilam*, an approach Dickey invites with his three epigraphs, one from Lucretius and two by Hume, which focus on the relationship of the individual to the physical universe as well as to himself. The materialist systems of Lucretius and Hume are juxtaposed with the idealism of other philosophers and then unified as Dickey develops the figure of "an Energized Man who unifies his own personality and thus unifies the two world views into a monistic *weltanschauung*" (6). Dickey describes this ideal individual in his essay "The Energized Man" as "the man with vivid senses, the man alert to the nuances and meanings of his own experience, the man able to appreciate and evaluate the relation between words in the right order ... and his perceptions and his mental faculties in *their* right order" (Weigl and Hummer 164). Like Nietzche's *ubermensch*, a figure who fully participates in the physical because he has integrated his perceptions and mental faculties, the energized man re-unites the materialistic and idealistic, an idea Dickey depicts in the characters of Frank and Joel Cahill.

The epigraph from Lucretius establishes Dickey's use of the air as the element in and on which airplanes move but also as the spirit which informs the mystical tradition, though Lucretius did not advance such a metaphysical aspect. The air's physical and metaphysical aspects reveal Joel Cahill's status as the energized man. A good pilot, he has instead become a mythic figure. Lucretius' *De Natura Rerum* poetically depicts a scientific perspective, a union of literature and science that Dickey reflects in Joel's aphorisms that imaginatively comment on the air and man's relationship to the universe. Dickey's use of Pythagorean ideas and their mystical focus on physical reality yields a metaphysical system in the novel that acts to counterbalance Lucretius. As a consequence of their exposure to mystically presented numbers, both Frank and Joel discern spiritual meanings beneath objective reality. Such "intensified awareness" (8) assists in their becoming "images of the Energized Man" (8). Frank Cahill becomes exposed to Pythagorean ideas while listening to Captain Whitehall's story concerning his role as navigator in a bombing mission, and these insights are enhanced with his initiation into the Alnilam group's use of the E6B computer. His son's ideas, then, begin Cahill's "reintegration of personality" (9).

Dickey's second epigraph, from Hume's *An Inquiry Concerning Human Understanding*, provides an additional materialistic perspective on experience and relates directly to Frank Cahill's blindness. Because he often misinterprets his impressions of the world, including the "wild doar," he learns to depend on intuition and instinct. Initially, he relies on Zack's instincts as well as his eyes, but gradually each becomes the focus of the other's instinctive faculties. By projecting his instincts through Zack, Cahill moves closer to the energized man who maximizes all his senses. Covel argues that the exhibitions of their power reveal a Nietzchean influence, a metaphysical aspect of his will to power that transcends physical strength. Cahill's physical strength consequently becomes joined with his integrated personality to effect "an objective correlative for his Will to Power" (12). That will to power most reveals itself when Cahill walks uninjured through the destructive confusion of the graduation ceremonies. Following this, he realizes that he no longer needs a guide dog. Just as Frank Cahill's physical presence represents the will to power, so does his son's spirit, which pervades the novel. Like his father, Joel also combines the physical and mystical world views. His personality is of such strength that he never appears in the novel, even though his presence motivates and leads the Alnilam group. His "metaphysical existence" (14) becomes reinforced both by his disappearance following his accident and by his supposed reappearance during the disruption of graduation, a return Covel likens to Nietzsche's idea of eternal recurrence.

Having located and identified himself in his metaphysical approach, Joel leaves the physical world; his actions then provide the answers to Dickey's final epigraph, a series of questions by Hume that express the broad search for identity. Joel situates himself in the universe through the E6B computer and the star Alnilam, but he transfigures both to a metaphysical level, thereby attaining a spiritual and physical position. Being blind, Frank Cahill discovers his place by questioning himself and others, having learned the unreliability of the senses. Dickey thus continually creates an intellectual tension between the idealist and the materialist philosophies, which serves to highlight the "the reassociation of sensibility" (16) that Frank and Joel Cahill experience as they become reflections of the energized man.

Dickey's novel-in-progress, *To the White Sea*, presents a sergeant, identified only as Muldour, who participates in a bombing raid over Tokyo during World War II. Shot down, he attempts by stealth, cunning, and cruelty to reach Alaska by means of the Bering Sea. Using first-person narration and divided into titled sections such as "Black" and "Orange," the present typescript is partly a character study, a psychological portrait of a man trained to kill by the exigencies of combat who becomes fascinated by violence. The work also concerns the idea of camouflage, the means by which Muldour identifies with nature by adopting not only its colors to survive but the qualities of motion and stillness, which assist this connection.

8: Other Prose: *Jericho, God's Images, Wayfarer,* and *Southern Light*

IN A 1974 ARTICLE discussing his efforts and those of painter Hubert Shuptrine to produce a major book about the South, Dickey declares,

> I want to write *how it feels to be in this place, the South. The essence of it. The mood of it. How it feels to be there on the coast ... to go there today and stand looking out over the marshes. And why it feels that way. Every place has its own quality of strangeness. Which is really uniqueness. That's what we want to capture. In paintings and words. The* feeling *of places.* (Logue 186)

Jericho: The South Beheld (1974), the book that resulted from the project initiated by *Southern Living*, was a commercial success and a critical failure. Following the publication in 1970 of *The Eye-Beaters, Deliverance,* and *Self-Interviews,* a book where Dickey examines his own life and poetry, he issued *Sorties* the following year, which contains his journals and several essays. All were intended for a scholarly audience. Critics consider *The Eye-Beaters,* published by Doubleday, and *Deliverance,* issued by Houghton Mifflin, major works, and *Self-Interviews* and *Sorties,* both by Doubleday, significantly address Dickey's own career as well as the contemporary literary scene in general. However, *Jericho* and *God's Images* (1977), published by Oxmoor House, the book division of The Progressive Farmer Company, are oversized books in which Dickey combines his writing with illustrations for a collector's edition market. Later volumes in the seventies also reveal Dickey's interest in this specialized audience: *The Enemy from Eden* (Lord Jim Press), *The Owl King* (Red Angel Press), *In Pursuit of the Grey Soul* (Bruccoli-Clark Press), and *Head-Deep in Strange Sounds* (Palaemon Press). These small publishing companies, often concerned with luxury editions, appealed to a less scholarly market than Dickey's major works.

Bowers-Martin (1984) sees the books published in the mid-seventies as transitional in Dickey's career. *The Zodiac* (1976) culminates his exploration of "transcendence through the idiom of the creative lie" (144), which constitutes his central thematic concern. Its "exaggerated horizontal shape" (144) suggests the large coffee-table books that immediately precede and follow it. Moreover, like *The Zodiac,* based on Barnouw's translation, *Jericho* and *God's Images* derive from other sources, the former from traditional Southern culture and the latter from the Bible. Yet *The Zodiac,* while logically grouped with Dickey's serious poetry because of its theme, also evidences the poet's interest in a specialized market. The poem's working manuscript was sectioned and bound into special-edition volumes; these Bruccoli-Clark collector editions were then sold by private subscription at $400 per book. Bowers-Martin, noting the specialized market intended by *Jericho* and *God's Images*, declares that neither book denies Dickey's theme of transcendence, but they explain the drastic turn in his publishing history. During the seventies Dickey failed to discover subjects and themes around which to create a new experimental poetry. Because *The Zodiac* concludes the poetic idiom he had been exploring, his inability to depict transcendence through a new technique led to *Jericho* and *God's Images*, which are "attempts to get extra mileage from what has worked before" (145).

Yet *Jericho* is only partly successful because Dickey fails to use "the main sources of his power" (145), including his own artistic control of the transcendent experience. In the introduction the poet asks the reader to become a "beholder," someone who can

> enter into objects and people and places with the sense of these things entering into him. What starts out as a deliberate act of attention ends as though he were not so much performing a rendition of Reality, but that a living action were being perpetrated on him.

While this approach poetically succeeds with "The Beholders" in *Falling* by fusing the personae and their surroundings, the implication in *Jericho* is that Dickey himself cannot impart "that energy, that transcendence" (145), particularly when he asks the reader to provide the imaginative vision requisite for such a fusion of inner and outer states: "You, reader, must open up until you reach the point ... of sensing your locality pour into you simultaneously through every sense." Dickey additionally eliminates the need for the creative lie, the very means by which he has previously provided transcendency and thereby given the reader, for example, a sheep child, two young lovers living in the mist around their wrecked motorcycle, a stewardess who lives only as she prepares to die, and blind children who attempt to see the origins of the race. In *Jericho* he takes traditional stories and asks the reader to view them in a heightened manner, an approach which undercuts his ability to lie creatively.

Dickey uses the persona of a seabird to view the South as the Promised Land. While hovering, swooping, or changing forms, the bird becomes whatever is necessary for each experience, but it always remains the same narrator, accompanying the reader in a series of "flickers." These experiences combine with actual landings as the bird touches Southern soil, a technique anticipated by the book's epigraph from Joshua: "Loose thy shoe from off thy foot; for the place whereon thou standest is holy." The first flicker occurs at St. Augustine, the South's oldest city, when the persona notices an oyster shell. Its condition, Bowers-Martin declares, establishes an important element in Dickey's fusion—the union of the natural and man-made worlds (146). Observing the shell, the bird says: "It is not lying on a beach, half-embedded in sand, but is jutting from a wall at an angle it never had in the sea." Such a conjunction is often repeated, as when the seabird flickers to Mobile's gardens: "No matter how close to them we are, no matter whether we help them grow or kill them, they are forever beyond us, these flowers." Southerners themselves exhibit this dichotomy in the way they lead their lives, partly grounded in their past dependence on the land and partly lived in an increasingly industrialized future.

Jericho concludes with a warning about the frailty of this fusion on which the new South rests. In Birmingham, Vulcan, the god of steel who provides the foundation for the Promised Land, says to the bird and the reader, "All this hardware I make: well, don't tell those new high-rising buildings of Jericho I told you; men used to call me Mulciber. You know what that means? The softener. They might get jittery. I might fall off this hill." Bowers-Martin believes this ending flicker reveals the elements of danger, repose, and joy that he also attempts to incarnate in his poems (147). Yet following these flickers, Dickey withdraws, leaving his audience to unify the experiences themselves: "Come down, reader, and be whole here."

Yardley's (1974) criticism seeks to define the larger nature of *Jericho,* asking whether the book is art or literature or "anything more than a colossal instrument" (43). Shuptrine's drawings are skillful, but they are also "imitative and sentimental" (43); Dickey's language "rolls" (43). Yet *Jericho* offers only a "sanitized and idealized" (43) South. Tailored to accommodate the readers of *Southern Living*, it is a book "for regional chauvinists to wallow in" (43), honoring only those qualities that affirm the Southern myth and ignoring those aspects that do not.

Critics quickly observed the extensive promotional campaign that accompanied the book's publication and which stressed not simply its size and Southern focus but also the magnitude of the sales effort. As Yardley does, they just as quickly faulted the content of *Jericho*. Evans (1975), for example, notes the book's big size (12 1/2 by 16 inches) and weight (7 pounds), its large first printing (150,000 numbered copies), and its extensive press release, which announced that the printing of *Jericho* required "28 carloads (one million pounds) of paper and 31 miles of cloth" (4). Such commercialism suggests "the poet decided to give himself over to the Alabama Chamber of Commerce" (4). Jones (1976) details the successful marketing strategy and campaign, arguing that the book's commercial popularity owes not only to the thorough testing and execution of a direct-mail campaign and the intense regional pride of Southerners but also to a national trend for nostalgia and a return to the land (250). Yet Evans, conceding that *Jericho* captures the South's haunted sense of pride and defeat, sees the failure to mention the Negro struggle for freedom as a major omission. Rather than presenting the civil rights movement, the book captures "the South that white Southerners think they live in" (4). Evans does acknowledge Dickey's awareness of the racial problem, citing his 1961 essay "Notes on the Decline of Courage." There he describes the black struggle as

> pointing up as nothing else in this country has ever done before, the
> fearful consequences of systematic and heedless oppression for both
> the oppressed and the oppressor, who cannot continue to bear such a
> burden without becoming himself diminished, and in the end debased,
> by such secret and cruel ways.... It is not too much to say that in the
> "Negro problem" lies the problem of the South itself. (*Babel* 258-59)

Later in *Self-Interviews* Dickey also states, "One must not be coerced ... into
writing about nothing but contemporary events; the larger forms of nature are
still there. Not only the Watts and Washington riots exist, but the universe
exists as well" (70). Dickey consequently is on "defensible ground" (5),
Evans believes, when choosing those experiences that move or interest him,
but *Jericho* is "an interpretative history" (5) whose announced theme is "The
South Beheld." That such a book omits the civil rights movement, therefore,
"shouts with Dickey's silence" (5). Furthermore, he omits discussion of the
decline of Southern values and specifically the region's new homogeneity.
The book's commercial success, despite these flaws, owes to the attitude it
promulgates, a nostalgia that confirms the white Southerner's view of himself
as a citizen in the Promised Land. It assures him that he lives in "a white
paradise without any recognition of a paradise lost" (5).

Lacking such a pronounced political focus, Donald's (1975) lengthy
review challenges the use of the word "collaboration" to describe the
Shuptrine-Dickey relationship since each traveled his own way through the
South by different means and recorded what each thought significant. As
Dickey writes, "We have made no attempt in this book to have paintings and
words coincide." Donald notes that, beside the obvious differences in their
portrayals, one visual and the other verbal, Shuptrine views the heart of the
South as the mountains, particularly those of North Carolina, since over one-
third of his paintings derive from these and another one-third from the
adjacent states of Virginia, Tennessee, Georgia, and South Carolina (185).
Dickey's scope is larger, "fourteen or so states," he writes, asking the reader
to follow in

> a gigantic spiral, going ... first along the Gulf Coast, through the
> bayous and over the Delta and the Great River, then into the huge and
> bewildering and heartening blue of West Texas, then north to
> Arkansas, through Kentucky and West Virginia and Virginia, briefly
> down to the South Carolina coast ... through Appalachia into Atlanta.

While Shuptrine's artistic focus is the countryside and country people,
Dickey concentrates on small-town life. As Dickey himself remarks,
Shuptrine is an artist "struck by *things*," while he himself excels not so much
with the trees, dogs, and dwellings of the South as with its people—the faith
healer, the bank robber, and the mill woman. Yet Donald believes both
artists share a common vision of the South as the Promised Land. Within
their respective mediums, what appears is their love of the land and the sense

that the idealized Southern life they present is dying or already dead. While containing humor, Dickey's language is "elegiac" (186), and his rhetoric, while celebrating the South, has "a dying fall" (186). These characteristics appear, for example, when he depicts the owner of a garden of azaleas: "He stands with both hands in the time-shade, bowed down with his money, exhausted with the income and upkeep of ancient Jericho, with the expense, the overhead of flowers, of old ladies fainting with vegetative rapture." Dickey more directly suggests the decline of the Old South when he writes: "This is a land of ghosts, and we feel nowhere come-truer than in a cemetery." Shuptrine's paintings express the same mood, the same sense of "a world in its final autumn" (186). Therefore, *Jericho* is not so much "a preview of the Promised Land but a nostalgic glance at Paradise Lost" (187).

Steadman (1975) faults *Jericho* both for artistic reasons and for its overstated assertion. While the text exhibits virtues of vitality, strong imagery, and a "sensual immediacy" (9), it nevertheless reveals a lessening of the intensity and sense of abandon that characterizes Dickey's poetry. Though Shuptrine's watercolors remarkably mirror Dickey's style, their concentration and emphasis on detail occasionally resulting in realism or something beyond realism, his paintings "do not penetrate beneath the visual to provide any deeper meaning" (9). Yet the book's principal danger lies in the reader believing *Jericho* more than it is, a problem Dickey compounds in his introduction by calling it "two deep views of Jericho, that will not come—or come together—again." The title, together with his statement that he and Shuptrine have "beheld" the South and offerred it with a "Biblical intensity," suggests that *Jericho* mythologizes the region more than it actually does. Dickey writes that the "landscapes, seascapes, mountains, rivers and people.... are our significance." However, the book fails both to depict the South's inextricable relationship with the past and, more importantly, to "cohere into a larger, expansive theme" (9).

More recent criticism, however, views *Jericho* as both a creative achievement and a product of Dickey's business acumen. Calhoun and Hill (1983) acknowledge Dickey's turn from his proclaimed mission as poet to a prose work intended for a popular audience and offerred by small publishing houses concentrating exclusively on luxury editions. The focus suggests either that Dickey was unable to explore familiar themes in creatively new poetry or that he could not finish *Alnilam*. The novel was finally published in 1987, but he had originally titled it *Death's Baby Machine* and detailed certain of its scenes as early as *Sorties* (1971). Yet this new direction also reveals Dickey's capacity "to 'make connections' with different kinds of readers" (121), showing many of the motifs previously apparent in his poetry, fiction, and criticism. *Jericho* depicts Dickey's Southern heritage, his ability to see clearly and poetically the details of the Southern landscape, and his "Agrarian love of the land" (121). The major change dictated by the new popular audience is Dickey's abandonment of "his role of poet of the expansive imagination" (121). No longer does he compel belief in situations and personae beyond the commonplace; rather, the reader assumes the imaginative task, instructed by Dickey to go "deeply into human life ... of our particular segment of the world and what it offers ... to those familiar with it by birth ... and those who come to the South as strangers." Perhaps because of the reversal of previously expected poet-reader roles, as well as the absence of the usual Dickey persona, *Jericho* succeeds only in parts; good images and inescapable scenes occur only infrequently. Calhoun and Hill additionally note the quantity of literary allusions, including ones to John Crowe Ransom, Allen Tate, and Donald Davidson as well as echoes of Dickey's own poems, a fact especially surprising since Dickey remains critical of "academicism" (122).

Like *Jericho*, *God's Images* (1977) has attracted almost no lengthy, critical study. Reviews were mixed, and later critics compare it unfavorably to *Jericho*. Less ambitious in size, though not in artistic intent, it contains fifty-three prose-poems that not so much re-interpret as re-present particular Biblical texts from individual perspectives. A similar number of etchings by Marvin Hayes accompany these re-presentations. Marty (1977) believes Dickey's text faithful in intent to the Biblical motifs it depicts, but while some passages are rich, others become too poetically sensual. Hayes's drawings, at once technical and imaginative, combine the literal with the visionary. When both artists "aspire least they accomplish most" (13). DeCandido (1978), however, considers Dickey's passages "oddly secular" (154), stating that they lack a "palpable spirituality" (154) because the emphasis shifts from God to the figures that present the Biblical story, characters moreover that are "predominantly masculine" (154). Admitting the prose is crafted and deeply felt, the review strikes a feminist approach, noting the absence of Judith, Esther, and Mary Magdalene from the portrayals and observing that Ruth and Mary are only "shadow and symbol" (154). *God's Images* narrows the Bible to "the worldly visions of two men" (154), a comment which ignores Dickey's own statements in the book's foreward:

> To an artist such as Marvin Hayes, or to a poet, such as I hold myself to be, these images have unfolded in us by means of the arts we practice. These are *our* images of *God's Images*.... These then, in this book, are some of the images from the inner kingdoms of two men.... Hayes and I do not wish to supercede or in any way substitute our interpretations of the Bible for yours. These are crucial to you, and therefore vital and living. We should like to think, though, that we may be able to give an added dimension to your own inner Bible and enrich your personal kingdom of God, there where it lies forever ... within you.

DeCandido fails to give Dickey the choice of his material.

Other reviews, however, were not influenced by political correctness. *Publishers Weekly* (1977), for example, states that Dickey's imaginatively subjective prose complements the etchings, which blend "realism with a disciplined sense of formal beauty" (Johnston 63). The reviewer notes the sincerity of both artists, particularly Dickey, whose effort was compelled by the death of his first wife, Maxine Syerson, a fact the poet acknowledges in the foreward: "She was all her life a devoted dweller in the Bible, and now, through the flowering tomb, she resides among the superhuman reality of God's images." *Booklist* (1977) and *American Artist* (1977) similarly see the collaborative interpretations of Dickey and Hayes as felicitous. The former asserts that Hayes's strength lies not only in his innovative approach to depicting well-known stories (the Crucifixion, for example, is shown as a reflection in Mary's tearing eye) but also in "the grace and economy of their realization" (344). Dickey lends this artistic interpretation an "emotional accompaniment" (344), often assuming the voice of the person he depicts, a technique which poetically reflects upon the visual meaning. This collaboration, *American Artist* observes, effects "a significant religious contribution for modern readers" (Preiss 26).

Oxmoor House, anticipating possible controversy from the book's unusual perspectives, established an advisory board of Biblical scholars, both Jewish and Christian, to assure that the portrayals were faithful to scriptural materials. Despite the offense taken by DeCandido, *Christian Century* (1977) sees *God's Images* favorably. Hayes's etchings bring a "new comprehension of biblical ideas" (1173), and Dickey's prose, "florid and reverent at once" (1173), reinforces the themes. Writing in *Theology Today*, Dillenberger (1979) raises questions about a literary work that depicts a religious subject. Hayes's etchings offer a series of select, dramatized vignettes, literally presented but without a comprehensive understanding of the Bible. Lacking such a unified overview, both artist and poet substitute piety. The illustrations sometimes evoke the theology of the sixties, as when in "Second Coming," Jesus becomes a tiny figure walking through a wide field of flowers. The "Crucifixion" has bathos, not pathos, although others like the "Death of Absalom" effectively present "the small, enclosed, compressed image which operates visually much as the epigram does verbally" (509). Many pictures, moreover, reveal an evasiveness about sexuality, with the figures seeming either castrated or purposely sexless, a troubling tendency since other sketches reflect the decade's more liberal attitudes. Too often, Dickey's prose passages must explain the disparity between the picture and the Scripture which accompanies it, breaching the incompatibilty as if the poet's role were interpretive. Dillenberger questions the relevancy of the panel of church experts whose names and credentials are listed in the frontmatter, suggesting instead a group of advisors from art and literature, because *God's Images* is literary, not theological, in its focus.

Calhoun and Hill (1983) view *God's Images* as more academic than *Jericho* because within Dickey's text lie the voices of Milton, Blake, and the translators of the King James Bible, not just certain past and present Southern poets. However, the varied narrations undermine the "conversational vigor" (122) inherent in a work with only a single narrator. Moreover, unlike *Jericho*, *God's Images* has no unifying thesis. Rather than trying to justify the ways of God to man, Dickey attempts to rework the images in his own poetic idiom. Trying to recover the common, unrecognized culture within his readers, however, Dickey actualizes Biblical images that, as he writes in the foreward, are "buried and live in us." While the poet in *Jericho* seeks to establish a shared Southern connection between poet and painter on the one hand and artists and their readers on the other, he endeavors in *God's Images* to broaden this intent to include Protestantism. Because of such purposes, both books become more than mere commercial enterprises.

Bowers-Martin (1984) extensively examines *God's Images*, both as it compares specifically to *Jericho* and more generally to Dickey's major themes and artistic techniques. Unlike Calhoun and Hill, she sees these books as a decided retreat from previous efforts. Dickey eliminates the need for the creative lie by randomly presenting stories with which the reader already is familiar and admitting in the foreward: "We all have our images of God, given to us by the Bible, which is the Word of God. These images are ours, and in calling them up in our minds we are living witnesses of the fact that 'the kingdom of God is within you.'" Yet in believing that his interpretation of the reader's personal images will engender a heightened understanding of each Biblical story, Dickey relies not on his own creativity but rather these preexisting stories. The fusion of the reader's inner state with the larger Kingdom of God, therefore, lies not with the poet but with his audience. Moreover, unlike the earlier book, *God's Images* lacks a unifying narrative voice; the episodes remain fragmented. In such poems as "The Sheep Child," "May Day Sermon," "Falling," and "Madness," the strong narrative voice compels belief by combining first-person immediacy with third-person objectivity, but Dickey now resorts "to whatever voice strikes him" (148). Sixteen of the twenty-nine Old Testament scenes use the omniscient narrator, while only six of the twenty-three New Testament episodes do, a statistic accounting for the former being the weaker section because it fails to provide what Lieberman ("Notes on James Dickey's Style" 1968) calls the feeling of "heightened reportage" (63). While exceptions to this in the Old Testament do exist, such as the account of Jacob's wrestling with an angel or of Joseph and the coat of many colors, these episodes for the most part fail to depict the fusion of inner and outer states. Each scene seems isolated and still, as if constrained within its own boundaries, an immobility that "negates the motion, the energy, that allows Dickey's best ideas to work" (149). Though the Old Testament section exhibits his main theme of transcendence, it remains "a gathering of fragmented thoughts" (149). The New Testament stories, however, allow Dickey more latitude to create the fusion of forces because Christ embodies the union of God and man. Additionally, Jesus is the speaker in five of the episodes and the subject of most others, which enables the reader to know him through experiences related by other voices. For example, Mary comments on her son's birth: "He is mine, or at least half of him is mine.... I cannot understand any of this, but I do know I hold in my lap a child who comes from me.... God needs a human mate to bring forth a human child." Christ possesses a double vision, seeing both into the world and beyond it, allowing him a serenity derived from knowing what other men through God may become. This attitude of becoming is the foundation of Dickey's work. He alludes to this theme in the foreward when he notes "the fabulous world we all have fallen from, and toward which we are always falling, not backward in time, but forward toward that moment when each story, each image of God will be found, will happen again."

In an interview in the spring 1976 issue of the *Paris Review*, Dickey refers to any effort other than poetry as a "spin-off" (Ashley 81), adding: "The main thing in poetry is the discovery of an idiom and the exploitation of it over an area of thought for a long period of time" (81-82). Bowers-Martin sees Dickey as successful here because the creative lie has remained the idiom through which he has successfully explored transcendence (150). However, in the interview Dickey also declares, "A poet's pages are filled up with what he's done, that he can live on and trade on; but he has *got* to find some way to love that white empty page, those words he hasn't yet said" (76). Here, *God's Images* fails because it does not fulfill Dickey's stated hopes as a poet. The scenes are merely "his old pages repackaged, and the process diminishes their quality" (151).

Dickey returns to the South in *Wayfarer: A Voice from the Southern Mountains* (1988), the subtitle indicating the continued use of his cultural and family heritage. The unnamed narrator greets a wayfarer he encounters at the book's opening. Superstitious and wise, he has lived his life in the Appalachians. When the traveler becomes sick, the narrator uses mountain medicines to restore his health, taking the wayfarer on a figurative journey as he talks about the food, geography, customs, handiwork, folklore, and music. He asserts, "We ain't got everything, but we got somethin'." As with *Jericho* and *God's Images*, the book is a collaborative effort, with William Bake's photographs not so much adhering to the story as cohering. The 178 pictures, primarily from the Southern Appalachians and particularly that section of the range from North Carolina, also strangely includes photographs from Texas and Oklahoma.

Reviews are almost nonexistent and generally superficial. Adams (1989) briefly compliments Dickey's "charming text" and Bake's "fine photographs" (120) and observes that the setting is appropriately never identified. Starr (1988) also views the joint effort as beneficial, declaring that the pictures reveal "an explorer's sense and an artist's eye" (1F) and comparing Bake to Monet and Wyeth. The people he captures belong only to the mountains; they are "constant, sturdy, quietly dignified" (1F). The pictures, however, are rarely correlated to Dickey's prose passages, most being grouped at the book's conclusion where they serve as "a visual epiphany" (8F).

Van Ness's (1989) essay-review more substantially discusses the book's dramatic development, declaring that *Wayfarer* "is not, or at least not only or even principally" (31) a coffee-table book. Bake's photographs create "an emotional immediacy," while Dickey's understated language presents truth as "an imaginative connection" (31), linking the reader to what the Appalachians are in and of themselves, "their spacial and metaphoric fullness" (31).

To do so, Dickey guides the reader on an heroic journey to recover what modern man has lost. As the narrator declares in "Departure," for example, speaking of mountain people, "They got ways of knowin'."

Dickey has always celebrated the individual who either begins over or who returns to a source and who must therefore relate what he has learned. That voice often appears suddenly in the narrative as the poet follows his own personae. Chance occurrences begin a poetic search for the forces that govern life, a search revealing "man's awful responsibility to drive toward self-discovery and self-determination" (32). The encounter between the anonymous narrator and the wayfarer, therefore, presents a familiar Dickey concern—the confrontation between an individual and a force larger than himself. In *Wayfarer* that other is the Southern mountains. While Dickey has poetically treated aspects of this subject before (for example, foxhunting and quilting in "Listening to Foxhounds" and "Chenille," respectively), the narrative framework of *Wayfarer* allows for greater breadth of treatment to depict what Van Ness calls "a larger natural inclusiveness in the world" (32). Consequently, when the speaker asserts, "It don't matter why it comes, but it does; it comes on through, and it's done been put into both of us, don't you see," Dickey moves beyond a discussion of family blood lines into "the lines of connection that link all men to the land and the natural impulses, the human need, to create and re-create what one sees and hears in the world" (32).

While *The Zodiac* and *Puella* also concern the artistic impulse and depict an individual seeking an exchange, *Wayfarer* differs in several respects. Not only does it attempt to have the visual and the verbal mediums interrelate, but its speaker also acts as an intermediary or guardian spirit, a guide who imparts to the adventurer certain protective amulets, as when the narrator gives the wayfarer a fairy stone shaped "like a cross" and which brings "good luck." As a result of his experiences, the traveler becomes "the new priest, a man who has been both outside and in" (32). His decision at the conclusion to speak for the first time, quoting Ransom's "Antique Harvesters," shows that he has undergone mythic rites of passage. Having crossed a threshold and penetrated forgotten truths, he poetically offers up what he has learned as he now prepares to return.

Southern Light (1991), Dickey's latest collaborative effort, attempts to capture through a poetic prose and the color photographs of James Valentine the distinctive qualities held in and projected by light. Valentine's 188 pictures dominate the book, which sections a day into dawn, morning, noon, afternoon, and evening and examines the world as light defines it during those times. In the introduction Dickey urges the reader to undertake the imaginative connection himself, a similar surrender critics like Bowers-Martin fault in his other oversized books. "Enter light," Dickey says,

> as though you were part of it, as though you were pure spirit—or pure beholding human creature, which is the same thing—to become part of light in many places and intensities, to make it something like

a dream of itself with you in it; that way you will be seeing by human light, as well as by the light shining since Genesis.

Unlike his previous mixed-media works, the prose text does not complement but anticipates Valentine's photographs. Their subtle textures and startling vibrancy demand confrontation, while Dickey's description establishes the uniqueness of the respective moments captured by the camera. When at dawn, for example, light causes the things of the world to come into themselves, Dickey invites participation by singling out what one might personally hold in perspective: "In all remoteness you have a hand, as everything sharpens, attunes: sharpens *toward*. If you want more leaves, beckon, and they come." In evening, he asks how successful the encounters have been and reminds the reader of the special quality of what light makes possible: "Nothing like it ever given, except by means of Time. This time, this day." The artistic intent seeks to allow a physical and emotional confrontation by having the words defer to the photographs and yet prepare one to experience them. Dickey establishes this collaborative dependency when, speaking of the creative impulse present throughout all human history, he states in the introduction: "The cave artist and the photographer, standing for all others, want to see not through but into: want you to stay with and *in* the work, and for it to stay with you, for it is in its very esence a form of ritual magic." While Dickey guides the reader's journey through the twenty-four hours *Southern Light* captures in words and pictures, he paradoxically remains less tangible a presence than in *Wayfarer*, despite his use of the imperative and despite the latter's narrative, which often subsumes Dickey's voice. However, as in all his efforts, his principal concern is the sense of consequence derived from human communion with the world.

9: Criticism and Belles-Lettres

IN A 1976 INTERVIEW Dickey states, "I don't believe that a reviewer can really criticize well unless he can praise well.... You've got to be able to like the right things to be enabled to dislike the wrong things" (Ashley 70). The comment mitigates the reputation Dickey quickly earned as the poetry editor of the *Sewanee Review*, where in the late fifties and sixties he challenged the work of established poets by questioning anyone he considered "suspect." To many, he seemed a "hatchet man," though his reviews contain little of the acerbic quality of Randall Jarrell's criticism. While judgmental, they are also entertaining. Scrutinized in retrospect, the reviews not so much present a consistent, broadly detailed philosophy as they highlight particular principles. They reveal, too, Dickey's attempt to distance himself from modernist poetry that, as he writes in *The Suspect in Poetry*, "brings into being a truly remarkable amount of utter humbug, absolutely and uselessly far-fetched and complex manipulation of language" (9). Rather, he seeks, too egotistically some contend, to create a "personal intimacy" (10) between the poet or his persona and the reader. In doing so, he explores "his own uniquely human segment of human consciousness" (55), extending it such that the reader participates in a shared understanding. The poet's self, then, becomes an "informing personality" (56) about matters of consequence.

Dickey collected many of his reviews from the *Sewanee Review*, *Poetry*, *The Hudson Review*, *The New York Times Book Review*, and *The Virginia Quarterly Review* and published them in 1964 as *The Suspect in Poetry*. The book's unity resides in Dickey's consistent approach to the poetry of the writers he considers—his belief that poems which seem artifically contrived or manipulated and that possess no relation to the world are "suspect" (9). In presenting his ideas and applying this standard to his enterprises, Dickey exhibits what Waggoner (1968) believes are Emersonian attitudes, expressions, and influences. Phrases such as "humanly perceived beauty" and "unliterary influence," as well as an emphasis on "experience" and "reality" that contrasts with linguistic "contrivances" (609), derive directly from Emerson's "The Poet." Moreover, Dickey consciously avoids references to such terms as "myth" and "vision" because he desires to separate himself from the modernist doctrine of Eliot and Pound, preferring instead a direct, unabashed search for "truth."

This quality of honestly seeking to confront truth as the physical world offers it leads Kostelanetz (1965) to label Dickey "the finest critic of American poetry today" (92). In *The Suspect in Poetry* Dickey directly examines insightful ideas and renders large, personal judgments, inviting argument or disagreement "as a pesty fly does a flyswatter" (93). For example, he declares the poems of Allen Ginsberg "a strewn, mish-mash prose consisting mainly of assertions that its author is possessed" (19). Of Thom Gunn, he asserts: "He performs endless labours to make simple ideas complex and important-sounding" (23). Dickey's straightforward sentiments derive from what Kostelanetz calls "honest fear and distaste" (93), the belief that poetry has become too false and that poets lie too much. Consequently, poems have become irrelevant to readers, judged but never experienced. That condition, Dickey states, is "too bad. Too bad for poetry, certainly, but worst of all for us" (11).

As a critic, Dickey assumes a poetic middle position between the academic on the one side and the anti-academic or "beat" on the other. This stance advocates a confrontation with life and yet holds forth the need for poetic form, a unity perhaps best characterized by "a synthesis of passion and intelligence" (Kostelanetz 93). Despite the fact that many of the best poets of the sixties emerged from this area, including John Berryman, Theodore Roethke, and Robert Lowell, Dickey's sense of contemporary poetry is "too ahistorical" (94). His concern with content fails to recognize the changes in form distinguishing this century's poetry from that of the previous, an emphasis that explains why he does not discuss writers like John Ashberry who extend the nineteenth-century tradition. Though Kostelanetz does not declare that Dickey intentionally omits discussion of form, he does assert that he "primes himself" (94), emerging from *The Suspect in Poetry* as "an innocent, honest, clear-eyed boy from the provinces" (94). Moreover, while his acumen and penetrating style result in substantive critical analysis, Dickey often becomes "too nice to bad poets" (94), following a harsh critique with a compliment. For example, in his review of Charles Olson's *Maximus* where he condemns the poem as inept and the theory behind it as flawed, Dickey then observes: "He has managed to write a few moderately interesting sections of a long, unsuccessful poem which must have been the labor of years, and these are worth reading" (31). Such an approving note ends almost every review, sounding discordant and giving him "an oafish image" (9) because the comments "probably symptomize his own uncertain feelings towards the critical position" (95). While Dickey views himself as a poet writing criticism, Kostelanetz would reverse the categories.

William Dickey (1965-1966) considers *The Suspect in Poetry* an unac-knowledged attack on academic poetry because of its failure "to talk about what is *real*" (614). While modernist poetry intellectually argues and philosophizes, such attributes lack relevancy to "the communication of poetic truth" (614), a belief apparent when Dickey dissects Ellen Kay's poetry:

One sees immediately that nature is never itself in Miss Kay's poems; nor does it belong to Miss Kay in any intimate and revealing connection. It belongs to the Proposition which it may be made to yield, if the poet rigs a satisfactory set of syllogisms.   (14)

Since man is most real, what William Dickey terms "poetic man" (615) when he involves himself in relationships resulting in "a fusion of singleness" (615), Dickey characteristically requires traits or qualities of the poet rather than of the poem. His prescriptions represent a Dionysian perspective. A poet honestly confronts reality and, compelled then to speak, he is overwhelmed by the poem even as he seeks an essentially religious communication. Such a view not so much affects intelligence as commitment, and Dickey consequently concerns himself less with the form the poetic utterance may take than with whether it liberates.

Dickey expands his examination of contemporary poets and poetry in *Babel to Byzantium* (1968). The volume reprints many of the reviews in *The Suspect in Poetry* and presents additional ones written in the fifties and sixties. Along with his critiques of sixty-seven individual poets and a short essay on anthologies, a second section more thoroughly discusses five specific poems Dickey believes important, essays which had originally appeared two years earlier as introductions in *Master Poems of the English Language*, edited by Oscar Williams. The three essays that comprise the book's final section, "Barnstorming for Poetry," "Notes on the Decline of Outrage," and "The Poet Turns on Himself," are similarly recycled from previous appearances either in anthologies or newspapers. The last of these pieces reveals the meaning of his title *Babel to Byzantium* and establishes his emphasis, consistent with comments he later makes in *Self-Interviews* (1970) and *Sorties* (1971), that each person possesses his own "spirit of poetry: the individually imaginative or visionary quality" (280) that constitutes his view of Byzantium. To realize this vision himself, Dickey endeavors to "incarnate my best moments—those which in memory are most persistent and obsessive" (292). While he endorses the poetic experimentalism of the fifties and sixties, he requires a proper balance between the passionate effusiveness of visionary poetry and the strict stylistics of formalist verse. To find his Byzantium, the poet must discover from within the cacophony of Babel a language uniquely his own that personally communicates a vision derived from "the inexhaustible fecundity of individual memory" (280). Most of the poets he reviews fail to accomplish this presentation of self.

Maloff (1968) sees the essays and reviews in *The Suspect in Poetry* as "fragments of a total structure" whose "organic design" (10) becomes apparent in *Babel to Byzantium*. Here Dickey records a continuing response both to contemporary poetry and to his own experiences as a man reacting vitally in the world. Feeling an urgency about his life, he becomes outraged by a bad poem not only intellectually and aesthetically but also morally; he considers it an affront. Because it is pretentious or trivial, it insults the spirit of what poetry ideally is, the means by which to humanize, illuminate, and transcend what Maloff calls "the beholder's inner life" (10). The merely clever and the academic equally incur Dickey's blame because both are badly told lies, and his analysis quickly identifies their faults—*these* lines, *this* image, *that* metaphor. He demands that the reader care intensely because such concerns affect the individual spirit. His insistent language suggests the "honesty and unstinting generosity of *self*" (10), a judgment repeated by Carroll in his essay-review "James Dickey as Critic" (1968). Carroll believes *Babel to Byzantium* reflects similar qualities to those in Dickey's poems—an insight unfettered either by literary fadism or by his own previous critical determinations and an originality whose imaginative power focuses on subjects that matter (82).

Dickey's reviews show a determination to avoid what is literarily popular and to argue only for those poets or poems he considers worthy, a critical independence that causes him to oppose, for example, the veneration offerred Charles Olson for his theory of "projective" or "open" verse, what Dickey refers to as "composition by field" (136). Conversely, he embraces minor poets like J.V. Cunningham, John Frederick Nims, Elder Olson, and Reed Whittemore and suggests that their means, though traditional or witty or dramatic, nevertheless are important because they craft with energy and care. Consequently, their voices and visions deserve consideration. Moreover, Dickey balances what he obviously dislikes in a poet with praise for what he sees as genuine. Carroll considers this ability to "transcend a fundamental antipathy" (84) as a "rare gift" (83) absent in most criticism, a quality that Kostelanetz (1965) disparages as critical indecisiveness. His best feature is his avoidance of a set of established criteria, a system of principles that serves to explicate and guide his analysis. Rather, Dickey explores only the "immediate, existential experience" (84) of the poem or poet he considers. Carroll systemically attacks what he refers to as "The Hunting of James Dickey" (85), the unfounded criticism of his works based on charges brought by Bly's essay "The Collapse of James Dickey" in the Spring 1967 issue of *The Sixties*. Little interested in closely reading such poems as "Slave Quarters" and "The Firebombing," Bly chose only to "bully poems into being flagrantly 'repulsive' examples of what he claims is their author's moral leprosy" (85-86). Continued denunciation of Dickey by Bly and his advocates suggests jealousy of his success as the first poet of his generation to publish both a collected poems (*Poems 1957-1967*) and a volume of criticism on modern and contemporary poets. Far from being self-serving, Carroll believes, Dickey lives and serves "the god of poetry and the god's faithful disciples" (87).

While Maloff and Carroll primarily discuss what Dickey says in *Babel to Byzantium*, Calhoun (1968) analyzes the nature of the criticism itself, particularly as it relates to the larger tradition of "polemics bordering on outrage" (75). Dickey wages primary battle against academic poetry, his perspective being "Dionysian, Whitmanesque, Lawrentian" (75). Yet his reviews lethally attack only Thom Gunn, James Merrill, and Allen Ginsberg and wound only Richard Wilbur because, despite his "rhetorical firepower" (76), Dickey sees mitigating qualities in almost all the poets he scrutinizes. His preface explains this lack of aggressive critical assault, stating that "any reasonably good teacher of aesthetics could tear his 'ideas' apart" and adding: "I abjure the full-scale critical performance, the huge exegetical tome that quite literally *uses up* the creative work it purports to discuss ... " (ix-x).

The disclaimer reflects the fact that the poet-critic offers little more than impressions in today's criticism because "the 'academic' critic can easily show himself more knowledgeable about existentialism, language analysis, linguistics, depth psychology, and myth" (76). Previous poet-critics of the twenties and thirties like T.S. Eliot and Allen Tate, as well as Randall Jarrell in the fifties, assumed important positions of authority because scholars had relinquished their literary responsibilities. Yet when Eliot recanted his stand on the efficacy of the poet-critic in *On Poetry and Poets*, such criticism lost its sense of legitimacy. While *Babel to Byzantium* lacks acute critical insight, Calhoun nevertheless believes it relevant to the poetry it examines. Though Dickey seems to promise a reassessment and even a ranking that remain unfulfilled, he does argue that contemporary poets are "long on skill but short on substance of the kind that communicates a meaningful experience to the reader" (77). Ideally, poets should remain suspended between "the extremes of freedom and restraint" (79), a position resembling the middle ground that Kostelanetz also discerns. Calhoun calls this mediation Dickey's "individualized version of the old rage-for-order concept, but the order is almost as important to him as the rage" (79). Because he does not believe in the autotelic poem, he tends to promote "a cult of personality" (80) in poetry, judging a work good if it reveals the poet's personality rather than that of someone he imitates. In addition to restoring a new "profound subjectivity" (80), Dickey demands substance and skill; with "voice" must be "vision." Only then, as Dickey declares with regard to Frost, will poems "come without being challenged into places in the consciousness of the 'average' reader that have seldom been visited before, and almost never by poems" (208).

"The Poet Turns on Himself" most clearly reveals Dickey's own method of discovering Byzantium and presents what Calhoun declares as the central theme of *Babel to Byzantium* as literary criticism—the relationship between the inner life of the poet and the poem he consequently creates (82). Never a formalist critic, Dickey consistently applies the concepts of sincerity and honesty to discover and define "the characteristic posture" (84) of the poets he reviews. He is therefore a moral critic, and while not a theorist, he is committed to pursuing what he believes the function and nature of poetry to be. Divided in his mind on poets like Randall Jarrell and Robinson Jeffers, he writes creatively in order to reach a final understanding. In his examination of Jarrell, for example, he divides himself into two separate speakers to conduct a dialogue between a critic's intellectual principles and a poet's emotional responsiveness. Such opposition, where criticism threatens enjoyment and intellect confronts emotion, structures the Jarrell essay but reveals Dickey's dilemma as a poet-critic, one which is responsible for his contradictions (88).

In *Self-Interviews* (1970) Dickey examines the development of his own career, explicating the origin and intent of many of his poems up through the publication of *Poems 1957-1967* and revealing the development of his creative psyche. Responding to questions tape recorded and then edited by

James and Barbara Reiss, he provides a volume that at times resembles autobiography. Calhoun and Hill (1983) observe that the confessionalism he avoids in his poems now seems "more acceptable to him in his own prose" (128). While uneven, the book decidedly refutes Eliot's formalism, the belief that poetry should be impersonal and the practice that carefully structured essays should promote the artistic form. Dickey insists on the value of the poet's own testimony concerning the origins, influences, and meanings of his work, thereby opposing such New Critics as Cleanth Brooks and Robert Penn Warren who believe that only a critic's close and objective literary analysis can expose the actual and not the intended meaning. What emerges in the volume is a descriptive and not a prescriptive analysis of his poetry and Dickey's strong belief in memory as a poetic resource—everything "that has come to the mind and become consciously or unconsciously assimilated or is in that strange limbo between conscious memory and the unconscious, where remembered things have what physicists call a half-life" (54-55). For Dickey, memory is likely "the only kind of wholeness we have" (57), and because he "cannot bear to believe these things will ever be totally expunged" (57), he writes to redeem the past and to energize the present with a passion and meaning it usually lacks. The emotions provide a sense of consequence. Dickey states: "I want to conserve the passion, wind it up tight like a spring so that it always has that sense of energy and compassion, that latency which is always available to anyone who looks for it" (65). Such a romantic principle opposes Eliot's dictum that the poet must find objective correlatives to which to transfer his personal emotions so that they transmute into impersonal artistic feelings.

Calhoun and Hill, however, argue that Dickey produces his own version of Eliot's dissociation of sensibility. Rather than a splintering between thought and feeling, Dickey views men as "deprived of instinctual life" (129), dispossessed from the primitive qualities that assured his survival. Modern technological specialization has resulted in what Dickey writes is "the loss of a sense of intimacy with the natural process" (68). To unify his sensibilities and achieve "a feeling of wholeness" (68), the individual must establish connections with the physical world, with "the great natural cycles of birth and death, the seasons, the growing up of other plants out of the dead leaves, the generations of animals and of men, all on the heraldic wheel" (68). Such intimacy permits good poems by enabling the writer to transcend the quotidian. Rather than being concerned with the wasteland, Dickey focuses on the natural world, believing along with D.H. Lawrence that "as a result of our science and industrialization, we have lost the cosmos" (67). Because *Self-Interviews* explores his poetic and philosophic beliefs and seeks to show how his own poems reveal these, the volume logically extends Dickey's analysis of other writers in *Babel to Byzantium*.

Wimsatt (1971), however, objects to the lack of profundity in *Self-Interviews*, declaring that Dickey's reflections fail to explore the emotional, psychological, or philosophical depths suggested by the poems themselves. Because he is primarily speaking or writing "hogwash" (502), his explications dissipate the strong performance achieved in his poems. Commenting on the sexual dilemma in "Adultery," for example, Dickey writes: "If there were any justice in the world, things wouldn't be that way. But there *isn't* any justice in the world in that sense, amd things *are* that way." Wimsatt labels such commentary "puerile" (502). Moreover, while she admires Dickey's diction, his use of periodic English as well as his fervent arguments for poetic autonomy, she believes he contradicts his own admiration for the instinctual by relating how hard and how long he works to create a line that says exactly what he wants.

Wimsatt's charge that Dickey lacks a philosophic understanding of the universe and that his critical explanations and judgments lack profundity is incongruous with the poet's wide range of readings and his minor in philosophy from Vanderbilt. The diction in *Self-Interviews*, owing to its spontaneous and oral method of composition, is informal; Dickey does not intend a philosophical treatise on the nature of literary criticism. Yet Aronson (1970-1971) also complains that "the gee-whiz tone of the whole still leaves one wondering" (464), asking how could "anyone who is self-aware say 'golly' about the darknesses Dickey's poems lead us into" (464). Moreover, he discerns a contradiction within Dickey's poetic belief of giving "the id free reign" (463) and his obsession with form and technique, stating additionally that when Dickey writes that his poems are less about what occurs than what he hopes might happen, he reveals "a curious lack of faith in the validity of his vision" (463). Calhoun (1971) considers the diction less effective than in *Babel to Byzantium*, the microphone not being conducive to producing either short barbs of stylistic wit or carefully worded introductory paragraphs, though *Self-Interviews* does capture Dickey's speaking tone. What surprises Calhoun is that Dickey's commentary offers so little one considers unexpected, as if the reader encounters "the public Dickey speaking on the level of good conversation" and not "the voice of the inner man" (11).

Sorties (1971) continues Dickey's artistic self-analysis, but the entries are undated prosaic ramblings written while actually engaged in creative efforts rather than taped conversation that retrospectively examines previous work. The statements are also more personal and intimate than *Self-Interviews*, and certain comments cause Calhoun and Hill (1983) to label the material "confessional" (130). For example, Dickey says of his drinking: "I have been drunk, more or less, for about the last twenty-five years. Everything I remember is colored at least to some extent by alcohol. What to make of this?" (84). He also confronts his mental fears: "I can't imagine going through such agony and terror, but I don't know where they come from, or if they come from anywhere" (73). Along with this "Journals" section, Dickey includes six essays and a short epilogue titled "One Voice."

Critical response to *Sorties* was negative. Particularly following *Self-Interviews*, the volume seemed to confirm that Dickey had ventured upon a self-chartered ego trip that promoted his memories and literary opinions as important, postmodern criticism. The large egocentric presence in his essays and his controversial public readings merely increased the perception that the poet only seriously considered himself. Moreover, Dickey had perceptibly failed to speak out against the Vietnam war, and liberals consequently viewed him suspiciously. Calhoun and Hill (1983) suggest that with the title of the book, Dickey views himself and his work as under seige. With the quantity of his poetry in decline, and according to some critics the quality as well, he was "apparently giving too much of himself and writing too little of literary consequence" (131). What appears most clearly in assessing the critical reception, however, is that in responding to *Sorties*, reviewers were unable to see past the author's personality to his work.

That personality consists of many Selves or stances. The macho Dickey who hunts with bow and arrow and champions the physical appears when he compares himself to his fictional creation in *Deliverance*: "I am Lewis; every word is true" (75). His emphasis on virility is just as direct: "The body is the one thing you cannot fake. It is what it is, and it does what it does. It also fails to do what it cannot do. It would seem to me that people would realize this, especially men" (4). The Whitmanesque intensified man who overreaches to embrace all life also appears in *Sorties*: "What I want to do most as a poet is to charge the world with vitality: with the vitality that it already has, if we could rise to it. This vitality can be expressed in the smallest thing and in the largest; from the ant heaving at a grain of sand to the stars straining not to be extinguished" (5). Dickey's role as a university professor, a seldom examined personality, reveals itself when he observes, "It is a marvelous thing, this having a house full of books" (5). His attack on academic poetry, a stance that earned him both admiration and condemnation, continues to assert itself. Entries throughout the volume support his philosophy that poetry should open up possibility. When Dickey declares that he does not "like the locked-in quality of formalist verse" (8), he advocates the idea that "the human imagination is wide—very wide indeed" (9). One consequently should create with "confidence, power, and relaxation" (9), though he refuses to abandon all form, telling himself: "To that, add precision" (9).

While *Sorties* presents an approach that, like his earlier criticism, is personal and subjective, differences from these antecedents appear. Calhoun and Hill discern a new interest in the lives of the poets he mentions, in what they call "the individual existential situations" (133) of other writers. In particular, he puzzles over the paradox between the affirmation of their poems and the destructiveness with which they live. The contradiction raises the issue of the relationship between the poet and his persona, a question Dickey addresses in his essay "The Self as Agent." The "I" in a poem is more than the ordinary self; it is the agent who enables the poet to discover his poem and thereby vitalize an aspect of himself. Because the poet is a varied personality, he remains "capable of inventing or of bringing to light out of himself a very large number of I-figures to serve in different poems, none of them obliged to act in conformity with the others" (161). Though Dickey provides no psychological justification for his theories, he consistently reiterates his position in the many forms his criticism assumes.

While reviewers acknowledge that *Sorties* reveals, sometimes perceptively, insights not only about Dickey and other poets but also about poetry itself, they usually focus on his too-large presence. Reeves (1972) believes that the book's primary value is not what it states about Dickey the man, despite the essentially private nature of a journal. Though generally favorable, the review observes that the book provides "a platform to Dickey the poet and Dickey the critic" (7). Norton (1972) more directly attacks Dickey, noting "the amazing amount of hypocrisy packed into 151 pages of what might be described as drippings from the poet's rather mundane existence" (10). What offends him is the contradiction between a poetry reading Dickey gave at Clemson University in the fall of 1971 when, drunk and incoherent, he received two thousand dollars for delivering "a blathering hodge-podge" (10), and an entry that reads: "I think too much of my body to offer it around to just anybody or to keep it un-lucid with drugs. Reality is drug enough for me" (81). Dickey's blatant egotism also offends Norton, who cites such statements as "it seems to me that I am the bearer of some kind of immortal message to humankind. What is this message? I don't know, but it exists" (54). Questioning why such a book would be published, Norton only concludes that Dickey hopes to provide an understanding as to how a poet thinks. What results, however, merely embarrasses, exposing "the explicit contradictions between Dickey the Culture Hero and Dickey the Man Growing Old; Dickey the Clean Sport and Dickey the Sensual Animal; Dickey the Immortal Poet and Dickey the Despondent Author" (11).

Kalstone (1972) also considers *Sorties* a critical failure, labeling it "little more than swashbuckling costume drama" (6). While journals belong to the private realm, this clearly beckons public consumption. Not only does Dickey use such offhand but audience-conscious statements as "to tell the truth," but he confuses literary dissatisfactions with entries intended to attract attention. For example, he groups Anne Sexton, Anne Stevenson, and Adrienne Rich and dismisses their efforts, assuming that their verse is indistinguishable. It is as if Dickey, under sustained attack, were "jockeying for position" (6) in an effort to secure his rank in contemporary poetry. Such posturing also suggests his frustration in actualizing his self. Oates (1974) observes in his poetry Dickey's consistent search for a personality in the midst of "intolerable truths" (99). Unable to discover himself, he abandons the effort at recreation by resorting to journals that Kalstone asserts "go public and missionary" (24).

Over a decade passed before Dickey published any additional criticism. *Night Hurdling* (1983) contains an assortment of writings, including poems, essays, conversations, commencement addresses, and afterwards. In the introduction, Dickey states, "Any collection of writings is an assertion of identity" (ix), and while certain that the variety presented suggests aspects of his self, he admits to being puzzled as to the precise nature of that personality. Rubin's (1984) brief review, representative of the continued critical neglect Dickey has received, states only that along with "much fustian" (23), *Night Hurdling* yields "some striking insights into poetry and poets" (23). While adverse reception to previous criticism may explain the lack of scrutiny in this regard, such oversight is unfortunate. Dickey's egotism and his large, invasive personality are notably absent when compared to *Sorties*, for example. Bowers' (1985) declaration that Dickey understands that "to get ahead in the marketplace the poet must know how to promote his product" (6) seems inappropriate here. Because of its eclectic offerrings, *Night Hurdling* does not promote any identifiable principle. As Dickey himself observes, "there are a good many threads here, all out of the same body. I don't have much of an idea as to where they lead, or if they weave themselves into a fabric, but they are the threads that have come" (ix). Confused himself, Dickey presents them "for whatever hint of insight—the making of a truth—they may contain" (xi). Like his poems, Dickey's criticism dramatizes aspects of the poet's ego and is not, as Calhoun and Hill correctly observe, "a self-contained or autotelic artifact" (134). The personal and critical essays, together with the poems, interviews, and afterwards collected by Dickey, reveal both the man as a writer and the writer as a man.

Conclusion

THE ABSENCE OF A collected edition of Dickey's poems has resulted in critical essays that primarily scrutinize a particular poem or volume of poetry. Only recently have book-length studies and extensive essays appeared that attempt to analyze and understand his larger career. The appearance in 1992 of *The Whole Motion*, which collects all his poems and contains a section titled "Summons" of previously unpublished or uncollected early poems, will provide the basis for a thorough examination of Dickey's development as an artist. A balanced assessment of the themes and techniques that characterize his different motions, including biographical and psychological considerations, remains, as do cross-genre studies. His children's poetry and *Alnilam* also require substantive criticism; neither has received the systematic study it merits. Finally, Dickey's creative efforts in translation also invite further work, though the lack of scholar accessibility to the language and idiom of Chinese, German, and French, among others, will likely restrict critical appraisal in this regard.

The editing and publication of Dickey's early notebooks, tentatively titled *Striking In*, should assist in evaluating the literary origins of his work. Critical studies have noted but not detailed the influences on his poetry, both those poets whom he began imitating, including George Barker and Roy Campbell, and those who seem to have impressed him later, such as Hopkins and Roethke. These studies might reveal new insights into his understanding of and experimentation with metrical techniques and imagery as well as a full understanding of Dickey's romanticism and the philosophical concerns and systems that underlie his work.

Dickey's place in the postmodern canon has yet to be decided. That he continues to explore creative possibilities renders futile any definitive understanding of his motion, but critical efforts should more fully establish its significance and continue to present its measure.

Bibliography

1. *Works by James Dickey*

Alnilam. Garden City, NY: Doubleday, 1987.

Babel to Byzantium: Poets & Poetry Now. New York: Farrar, Strauss, & Giroux, 1968.

Bronwen, the Traw, and the Shape-Shifter. San Diego, New York, and London: Bruccoli Clark and Harcourt Brace Jovanovich, 1986.

Buckdancer's Choice. Middletown, CT: Wesleyan University Press, 1965.

The Central Motion: Poems, 1968-1979. Middletown, CT: Wesleyan University Press, 1983.

Deliverance. Boston: Houghton Mifflin, 1970.

Drowning With Others. Middletown, CT: Wesleyan University Press, 1962.

The Eagle's Mile. Hanover and London: Wesleyan University Press and University Press of New England, 1990.

The Early Motion: Drowning With Others and Helmets. Middletown, CT: Wesleyan University Press, 1981.

The Eye-Beaters, Blood, Victory, Madness, Buckhead and Mercy. Garden City, NY: Doubleday, 1970.

Falling, May Day Sermon, and Other Poems. Middletown, CT: Wesleyan University Press, 1981.

God's Images: The Bible: A New Vision. Birmingham, AL: Oxmoor House, 1977.

Helmets. Middletown, CT: Wesleyan University Press, 1964.

Into the Stone and Other Poems, in *Poems of Today VII*, ed. John Hall Wheelock. New York: Scribner's, 1960.

Jericho: The South Beheld. Birmingham, AL: Oxmoor House, 1974.

Night Hurdling: Poems, Essays, Conversations, Commencements, and Afterwards. Columbia, SC and Bloomfield Hills, MI: Bruccoli Clark, 1983.

Poems, 1957-1967. Middletown, CT: Wesleyan University Press, 1967.

Puella. Garden City, NY: Doubleday, 1982.

Self-Interviews. Garden City, NY: Doubleday, 1970.

Sorties. Garden City, NY: Doubleday, 1971.

Southern Light. Birmingham, AL: Oxmoor House, 1991.

The Strength of Fields. Garden City, NY: Doubleday, 1979.

The Suspect in Poetry. Madison, MN: Sixties Press, 1964.

Tucky the Hunter. New York: Crown, 1978.

Wayfarer: A Voice from the Southern Mountains. Birmingham, AL: Oxmoor House, 1988.

The Zodiac. Garden City, NY: Doubleday, 1976.

2. Critical Works

Adams, Percy. "The Epic Tradition and the Novel." *Southern Review* NS 9 (Spring 1973): 300-310.

Adams, Phoebe-Lou. "*Wayfarer.*" *Atlantic Monthly* 263 (January 1989): 120.

Anderson, Mia. "A Portrait of the Artist as White-Water Canoeist." *James Dickey Newsletter* 2 (Spring 1986): 11-16.

Applewhite, James. "Reflections on *Puella.*" *Southern Review* 21 (January 1985): 214-19.

Armour, Robert. "*Deliverance*: Four Variations of the American Adam." *Literature / Film Quarterly* 1 (July 1973): 280-85.

Arnett, David L. "An Interview with James Dickey." *Contemporary Literature* 16 (Summer 1975): 286-300.

Aronson, James. "*Self-Interviews.*" *Antioch Review* 30 (Fall/Winter 1970-71): 463-64.

Ashley, Franklin. "James Dickey: The Art of Poetry XX." *Paris Review* 65-68 (Spring 1976): 52-88.

Balakian, Peter. "Poets of Empathy." *Literary Review: An International Journal of Contemporary Writing* 27, no.1 (1983): 135-46.

Barshay, Robert. "Machismo in *Deliverance*." *Teaching English in the Two-Year College* 1, no.3 (1975): 169-73.

Baughman, Ronald. "In Dickey's Latest, Blindness Opens a Man's Eyes to Life." *The Philadelphia Inquirer*. 31 May 1987. S1, S8.

—. "James Dickey's *The Eye-Beaters*: 'An Agonizing New Life'." *South Carolina Review* 10 (April 1978): 81-88.

—. "James Dickey's War Poetry: A 'Saved, Shaken Life'." *South Carolina Review* 15 (April 1983): 38-48.

—. *Understanding James Dickey*. Columbia: U of South Carolina Press, 1985.

Beidler, Peter G. "'The Pride of Thine Heart Hath Deceived Thee:' Narrative Distortion in Dickey's *Deliverance*." *South Carolina Review* 3 (December 1972): 29-40.

Bennett, Joseph. "A Man With a Voice." *New York Times Book Review*. 6 February 1966. 10.

Bennett, Ross. "'The Firebombing': A Reappraisal." *American Literature* 52 (November 1980): 430-48.

Berke, Roberta. *Bounds Out of Bounds: A Compass for Recent American and British Poetry*. New York: Oxford U Press, 1981.

Berry, David. "Harmony with the Dead: James Dickey's Descent into the Underworld." *Southern Quarterly* 12 (April 1974): 233-44.

Berry, Wendell. "James Dickey's New Book." *Poetry* 105 (November 1964): 130-31.

Bloom, Harold. "James Dickey: From 'The Other' through *The Early Motion*." *Southern Review* 21 (January 1985): 63-78.

Bly, Robert. "The Collapse of James Dickey." *The Sixties* (Spring 1967): 70-79.

—. "The Work of James Dickey." *The Sixties* (Winter 1964): 41-57.

Bobbitt, Joan. "Unnatural Order in the Poetry of James Dickey." *Concerning Poetry* 11 (Spring 1978): 39-44.

Booklist. "*God's Images: The Bible: A New Vision*." 74 (15 October 1977): 344.

Bornhouser, Fred. "Poetry by the Poem." *Virginia Quarterly Review* 41 (Winter 1965): 146-52.

Bowers, Neal. *James Dickey: The Poet as Pitchman*. Columbia: U of Missouri Press, 1985.

Bowers-Hill, Jane. "'With Eyes Far More Than Human': Dickey's Misunderstood Monster." *James Dickey Newsletter* 1 (Fall 1984): 2-8.

Bowers-Martin, Jane. "*Jericho* and *God's Images*: The Old Dickey Theme." In Weigl and Hummer 143-51.

Brewer, Angelin. "'To Rise above Time:' The Mythic Hero in Dickey's *Deliverance* and *Alnilam*." *James Dickey Newsletter* 7 (Fall 1990): 9-14.

Bruccoli, Matthew J., ed. *Pages: The World of Books, Writers, and Writing*. Detroit: Gale Research, 1976.

Burnshaw, Stanley. "Star-Beasts of Intellect and Madness: *The Zodiac*." *Book World*. 21 November 1976. E1.

Calhoun, Richard J. "After a Long Silence: James Dickey as South Carolina Writer." *South Carolina Review* 9 (November 1976): 12-20.

—. "'His Reason Argues With His Invention'—James Dickey's *Self-Interviews* and *The Eye-Beaters*." *South Carolina Review* 3 (June 1971): 9-16.

—. "Whatever Happened to the Poet-Critic?" *Southern Literary Journal* 1 (Autumn 1968): 75-88.

Calhoun, Richard J., and Robert W. Hill. *James Dickey*. Boston: Twayne, 1983.

Calhoun, Richard J., ed. *James Dickey: The Expansive Imagination: A Collection of Critical Essays*. DeLand, FL: Everett/Edwards, 1973.

Carnes, Bruce. "Deliverance in James Dickey's 'On the Coosawattee' and *Deliverance*." *Notes on Contemporary Literature* 7 (March 1977): 2-4.

Carroll, Paul. "James Dickey as Critic: *Babel to Byzantium*." *Chicago Review* 20 (November 1968): 82-87.

—. *The Poem In Its Skin*. Chicago: Big Table Publishing Company, 1968.

—, ed. *The Young American Poets*. Chicago: Big Table Publishing Company, 1968.

Cassity, Turner. "Double Dutch: *The Strength of Fields* and *The Zodiac*." *Parnassus: Poetry in Review* (Spring/Summer 1981): 177-93.

Cavell, Marcia. "Visions of Battlements." *Partisan Review* 38, no.1 (1971): 117-21.

Chappell, Fred. "Dickey Novel Wordy, but Not Boring." *The State*. 21 June 1987. 6F.

—. "Vatic Poesy." *The State*. 9 December 1991. 5F.

Christian Century. "Books of the Season." 94 (14 December 1977): 1173.

Clausen, Christopher. "Grecian Thoughts in the Home Fields: Reflections on Southern Poetry." *Georgia Review* 32 (Summer 1978): 283-305.

Connell, Evan S. "*Deliverance*." *New York Times Book Review*. 22 March 1970. 1, 23.

Corrington, John William. "James Dickey's *Poems 1957-1967*: A Personal Appraisal." *Georgia Review* 22 (Spring 1968): 12-23.

Covel, Robert C. "The Metaphysics of Experience: James Dickey's 'The Scarred Girl'." *James Dickey Newsletter* 1 (Spring 1985): 24-30.

—. "'A Starry Place': The Energized Man in Dickey's *Alnilam*." *James Dickey Newsletter* 5 (Spring 1989): 5-17.

Davis, Charles E. "The Wilderness Revisited: Irony in James Dickey's *Deliverance*." *Studies in American Fiction* 4 (Autumn 1976): 223-30.

Davison, Peter. "The Difficulties of Being Major: The Poetry of Robert Lowell and James Dickey." *Atlantic Monthly* 220 (October 1967): 116-21.

DeCandido, GraceAnne A. "*God's Images: The Bible—A New Vision*." *Library Journal* 103 (15 January 1978): 154.

De La Fuente, Patricia, ed. *James Dickey: Splintered Sunlight*. Edinburg, TX: Pan American University, 1979.

DeMott, Benjamin. "The 'More Life' School and James Dickey." *Saturday Review* (28 March 1970): 25-26, 38.

Dickey, William. "Talking About What's Real." *Hudson Review* 18 (Winter 1965-66): 613-17.

Dillenberger, Jane. "*God's Images: The Bible: A New Vision*." *Theology Today* 35 (January 1979): 507-11.

Donald, David Herbert. "Promised Land or Paradise Lost: The South Beheld." *Georgia Review* 29 (Spring 1975): 184-87.

Donoghue, Denis. "The Good Old Complex Fate." *Hudson Review* 17 (Summer 1964): 267-77.

Doughtie, Edward. "Art and Nature in *Deliverance.*" *Southwest Review* 64 (Spring 1979): 167-80.

Duncan, Robert. "Oriented by Instinct by Stars." *Poetry* 105 (November 1964): 131-33.

Edwards, C. Hines. "Dickey's *Deliverance*: The Owl and the Eye." *Critique: Studies in Modern Fiction* 15, no.2 (1973): 95-101.

—. "Initiation Ritual in 'The Shark's Parlor'." *James Dickey Newsletter* 7 (Spring 1991): 19-23.

Evans, Eli N. "The South the South Sees: *Jericho.*" *New York Times Book Review.* 9 February 1975. 4-5.

Eyster, Warren. "Two Regional Novels." *Sewanee Review* 79 (Summer 1971): 469-74.

Filler, Louis, ed. *Seasoned Authors for a New Season: The Search for Standards in Popular Writing.* Bowling Green, OH: Bowling Green University Popular Press, 1980.

Fraser, G.S. "The Magicians." *Partisan Review* 38 (1971-72): 469-78.

Friedman, Norman. "The Wesleyan Poets—II." *Chicago Review* 19 (January 1966): 55-67, 72.

Glancy, Eileen. *James Dickey: The Critic as Poet.* Troy, NY: Whitson, 1971.

Gregor, Arthur. "James Dickey, American Romantic." In Calhoun 77-80.

Greiner, Donald J. "The Harmony of Bestiality in James Dickey's *Deliverance.*" *South Carolina Review* 5 (December 1972): 43-49.

Guillory, Daniel L. "Myth and Meaning in James Dickey's *Deliverance.*" *College Literature* 3 (1976): 56-62.

—. "Water Magic in the Poetry of James Dickey." *English Language Notes* 8 (December 1970): 131-37.

Guttenberg, Barnett. "The Pattern of Redemption in Dickey's *Deliverance.*" *Critique: Studies in Modern Fiction* 18, no.3 (1977): 83-91.

Haule, James M. "'The Thing Itself Is in That': Closure in the Poetry of James Dickey." In De La Fuente 31-44.

Heilbrun, Carolyn. "The Masculine Wilderness of the American Novel." *Saturday Review* (29 January 1982): 41-44.

Heylen, Romy. "James Dickey's *The Zodiac*: A Self-Translation?" *James Dickey Newsletter* 6 (Spring 1990): 2-17.

Hill, Robert W. "James Dickey: Comic Poet." In Calhoun 143-55.

Hodge, Marion. "James Dickey's Natural Heaven and the Tradition." *James Dickey Newsletter* 7 (Fall 1990): 15-21.

—. "The New King at Dover." *James Dickey Newsletter* 2 (Fall 1985): 17-20.

Hollahan, Eugene. "An Anxiety of Influence Overcome: Dickey's *Puella* and Hopkins' *The Wreck of the 'Deutschland'*." *James Dickey Newsletter* 1 (Spring 1985): 2-12.

Holley, Linda Tarte. "Design and Focus in James Dickey's *Deliverance*." *South Carolina Review* 10 (April 1978): 90-98.

Howard, Richard. "On James Dickey." *Partisan Review* 33 (Summer 1966): 414-28, 479-86.

Italia, Paul G. "Love and Lust in James Dickey's *Deliverance*." *Modern Fiction Studies* 21 (Summer 1975): 203-13.

Jameson, Fredric. "The Great American Hunter, or, Ideological Content in the Novel." *College English* 34 (November 1972): 180-97.

Johnston, Albert H. "*God's Images: The Bible—A New Vision*." *Publishers Weekly* 212 (15 August 1977): 63.

—. "*Tucky the Hunter*." *Publishers Weekly* 214 (31 July 1978): 88.

Jolly, John. "Drew Ballinger as 'Sacrificial God' in James Dickey's *Deliverance*." *South Carolina Review* 17 (Spring 1985): 102-8.

Jones, Betty Ann. "*Jericho*: The Marketing Story." In Bruccoli 248-53.

Kalstone, David. "*Sorties*." *New York Times Book Review*. 23 January 1972. 6, 24.

Kennedy, X.J. "Joys, Griefs, and 'All Things Innocent, Hapless, Forsaken'." *New York Times Book Review*. 23 August 1964. 5.

—. "Sometimes It's the Sound That Counts." *New York Times Book Review*. 15 July 1962. 4.

Kerley, Gary. "Dickey Delivers Second Novel." *Gainesville Times*. 19 July 1987. 5E.

—. "Understanding 'This Hunter Made Out of Stars': The Myth of Orion in James Dickey's *Alnilam*." *James Dickey Newsletter* 4 (Fall 1978): 15-22.

—. "Unifying the Energy and Balancing the Vision: Nature, Man, and Quest in James Dickey's *Deliverance* and *Alnilam*." *James Dickey Newsletter* 5 (Spring 1989): 17-26.

Kirkus. "*Bronwen, the Traw, and the Shape-Shifter*." 54 (15 August 1986): 1289-90.

—. "*Tucky the Hunter*." 46 (15 August 1978): 917.

Kirschten, Robert. *James Dickey and the Gentle Ecstasy of Earth*. Baton Rouge: Louisiana State U Press, 1988.

—, ed. *James Dickey: Critical Essays in American Literature*. New York: G.K. Hall. Forthcoming.

Korges, James. "James Dickey and Other Good Poets." *Minnesota Review* 3 (Summer 1963): 473-91.

Kostelanetz, Richard. "Flyswatter and Gadfly." *Shenandoah* 16 (Spring 1965): 92-95.

Kunz, Don. "Learning the Hard Way in James Dickey's *Deliverance*." *Western American Literature* 12 (February 1978): 289-301.

Landess, Thomas. "Traditional Criticism and the Poetry of James Dickey." *Occasional Review* 3 (Summer 1975): 5-26.

Lask, Thomas. "Serene and Star-Crazed." *New York Times*. 22 January 1977. 19.

Leibowitz, Herbert. "The Moiling of Secret Forces: *The Eye-Beaters, Blood, Victory, Madness, Buckhead and Mercy*." *New York Times Book Review*. 8 November 1970. 20, 22.

Lensing, George. "James Dickey and the Movements of Imagination." In Calhoun 157-75.

Lensing, George S. "The Neo-Romanticism of James Dickey." *South Carolina Review* 10 (April 1978): 20-32.

Lieberman, Laurence. *The Achievement of James Dickey*. Glenview, IL.: Scott, Foresman and Company, 1968.

—. "Exchanges: Inventions in Two Voices: *The Strength of Fields*." *Sewanee Review* 88 (Summer 1980): lxv-lxvi.

—. "James Dickey—The Deepening of Being." In Lieberman 1-21.

—. "Notes on James Dickey's Style." *The Far Point* 2 (Spring/Summer 1968): 57-63.

—. "The Worldly Mystic." *Hudson Review* 20 (Autumn 1967): 513-20.

Lindborg, Henry J. "James Dickey's *Deliverance*: The Ritual of Art." *Southern Literary Journal* 6 (Spring 1974): 83-90.

Literature as Revolt and Revolt as Literature: Three Studies in the Rhetoric of Non-Oratorical Forms. Minneapolis: Proceedings of the Fourth Annual University of Minnesota Spring Symposium in Speech-Communication, 1969.

Logue, J.D. "Books About the South." *Southern Living* 9 (February 1974): 184, 186.

—. "Books About the South." *Southern Living* 14 (January 1979): 68.

Longen, Eugene M. "Dickey's *Deliverance*: Sex and the Great Outdoors." *Southern Literary Journal* 9 (Spring 1977): 137-49.

Macaulay, David. "*Bronwen, the Traw, and the Shape-Shifter.*" *New York Times Book Review.* 8 March 1987. 31.

Maloff, Saul. "Poet Takes His Turn as Critic: *Babel to Byzantium.*" *Book World.* 30 June 1968. 10.

Mapp, Joy E. "James Dickey's 'The Eye-Beaters': The Savage Spear of Salvation." *James Dickey Newsletter* 8 (Spring 1992): 27-35.

Marin, Daniel B. "James Dickey's *Deliverance*: Darkness Visible." *South Carolina Review* 3 (November 1970): 49-59.

Markos, Donald W. "Art and Immediacy: James Dickey's *Deliverance.*" *Southern Review* NS 7 (Summer 1971): 947-53.

Marty, Martin E. "God and Man: *God's Images.*" *New York Times Book Review.* 18 December 1977. 13.

Martz, William J. "A Note on Meaningless Being in 'Cherrylog Road'." In Calhoun 81-83.

Mason, Kenneth C. "A Book to Relish." *Prairie Schooner* 54 (Winter 1980-81): 107-8.

McGinnis, Wayne D. "Mysticism in the Poetry of James Dickey." *New Laurel Review* 5, nos.1-2 (1975): 5-10.

McNamara, Eugene. "James Dickey's 'The Eye-Beaters': Poetry of the Burning Bush." *James Dickey Newsletter* 3 (Fall 1986): 20-24.

Medwick, Cathleen. "Moby Dickey." *Vogue* (June 1987): 118, 120.

Meredith, William. "A Good Time for All: *Poems 1957-1967.*" *New York Times Book Review.* 23 April 1967. 4, 46.

Metz, Violette. "The Blessed Beasts and Children: An Examination of Imagery in James Dickey's *Poems 1957-1967.*" In De La Fuente 45-55.

Mills, Ralph J. *Creation's Very Self: On the Personal Element in Recent American Poetry.* Fort Worth: Texas Christian U Press, 1969.

—. *Cry of the Human: Essays on Contemporary American Poetry.* Urbana, Chicago, and London: U of Illinois Press, 1975.

—. "The Poetry of James Dickey." *TriQuarterly* 11-14 (Winter 1968): 231-42.

Mitgang, Herbert. "Man, Nature and Everyday Activities in Verse." *New York Times.* 27 October 1990. 16.

Mizejewski, Linda. "Shamanism Toward Confessionalism: James Dickey, Poet." *Georgia Review* 32 (Summer 1978): 409-19.

Monk, Donald. "Colour Symbolism in James Dickey's *Deliverance.*" *Journal of American Studies* 11, no.2 (1977): 261-79.

Morris, Christopher. "Dark Night of the Flesh: the Apotheosis of the Bestial in James Dickey's *The Zodiac.*" *Contemporary Poetry* 4, no.4 (1982): 31-47.

Morris, Harry. "A Formal View of the Poetry of Dickey, Garrigue, and Simpson." *Sewanee Review* 77 (Spring 1969): 318-25.

Nemerov, Howard. "Poems of Darkness and a Specialized Light." *Sewanee Review* 71 (Winter 1963): 99-104.

Niflis, N. Michael. "A Special Kind of Fantasy: James Dickey on the Razor's Edge." *Southwest Review* 57 (Autumn 1972): 311-17.

Norton, John. "Ego-tripping with James Dickey." *Osceola* (23 May 1972): 10-11.

Oates, Joyce Carol. "Out of Stone into Flesh: The Imagination of James Dickey." *Modern Poetry Studies* 5, no.2 (1974): 97-144.

Pair, Joyce. "'Dancing With God': Totemism in Dickey's 'May Day Sermon'." In Kirschten, ed.

Parini, Jay. "James Dickey's Massive and Mystifying *Alnilam.*" *USA Today.* 29 May 1987. 70.

Peterman, Gina. "The Clothing Metaphor in James Dickey's 'Springer Mountain' and 'Falling'." *James Dickey Newsletter* 7 (Spring 1991): 12-18.

Peters, Robert. "The Phenomenon of James Dickey, Currently." *Western Humanities Review* 34 (Spring 1980): 159-66.

Pierce, Constance. "Dickey's 'Adultery': A Ritual of Renewal." *Concerning Poetry* 9, no.2 (1976): 67-69.

Playboy. "Review of *Alnilam*." 34 (August 1987): 25.

Preiss, David. "Art Books." *American Artist* 41 (November 1977): 26.

Prescott, Peter S. "Lost in the Stars: *The Zodiac*." *Newsweek* 88 (6 December 1976): 89.

Ramsey, Paul. "James Dickey: Meter and Structure." In Calhoun 177-94.

Reeves, Garland. "Poet's Perspective Journal Criticizes Works of Others." *Birmingham News*. 13 February 1972. E7.

Rose, Maxine S. "On Being Born Again: James Dickey's 'May Day Sermon to the Women of Gilmer County, Georgia, by a Woman Preacher Leaving the Baptist Church'." *Research Studies* 46 (December 1978): 254-58.

Rosenthal, M.L. *The New Poets: American and British Poetry Since World War II*. New York: Oxford U Press, 1967.

Rubin, Louis D. "Rituals of Risk." *New York Times Book Review*. 3 June 1984. 23.

Schechter, Harold. "The Eye and the Nerve: A Psychological Reading of James Dickey's *Deliverance*." In Filler 4-19.

Schmitt, Ronald. "Transformations of the Hero in James Dickey's *Deliverance*." *James Dickey Newsletter* 8 (Fall 1991): 9-16.

Seale, Jan. "Narrative Technique in James Dickey's 'May Day Sermon'." In De La Fuente 24-30.

Shaw, Robert B. "Poets in Midstream." *Poetry* 118 (July 1971): 228-33.

Silverstein, Norman. "James Dickey's Muscular Eschatology." *Salmagundi* 22-23 (Spring/Summer 1973): 258-68.

Skinner, Izora. "A Fun Poem by James Dickey." In De La Fuente 56-58.

Skipp, Francis. "James Dickey's *The Zodiac*: The Heart of the Matter." *Concerning Poetry* 14, no.1 (1981): 1-10.

Sloan, Thomas O. "The Open Poem Is a Now Poem: Dickey's 'May Day Sermon'." In *Literature as Revolt and Revolt as Literature: Three Studies in the Rhetoric of Non-Oratorical Forms* 17-31.

Smith, Dave. "The Strength of James Dickey." *Poetry* 137 (March 1981): 349-58.

Smith, Mack. "James Dickey's Varieties of Creation: The Voices of Narrative." *James Dickey Newsletter* 1 (Spring 1985): 18-22.

Smith, Raymond. "The Poetic Faith of James Dickey." *Modern Poetry Studies* 2, no.1 (1972): 259-72.

Spears, Monroe. *Dionysus and the City: Modernism in Twentieth-Century Poetry.* New York: Oxford U Press, 1970.

—. "James Dickey as a Southern Visionary." *Virginia Quarterly* 63 (Winter 1987): 110-23.

Sporborg, Ann. *"Bronwen, the Traw, and the Shape-Shifter."* *James Dickey Newsletter* 4 (Fall 1987): 25-28.

Starr, William W. "James Dickey's Novel Explores Father and Son Relationships." *The State.* 17 May 1987. 1F, 10F.

—. "The Title Fight." *The State.* 16 October 1988. 1F, 8F.

Steadman, Venson. "A Skillful Tribute, Nothing More: *Jericho: The South Beheld.*" *Osceola* (14 February 1975): 9.

Steinberg, Sybil. *"Alnilam."* *Publishers Weekly* 231 (17 April 1987): 65.

Stepanchev, Stephen. *American Poetry Since 1945.* New York: Harper & Row, 1965.

Strange, William C. "To Dream, To Remember: James Dickey's *Buckdancer's Choice.*" *Northwest Review* 7 (Fall/Winter 1965-66): 33-42.

Strong, Paul. "James Dickey's Arrow of Deliverance." *South Carolina Review* 11 (November 1978): 108-16.

Taylor, Chet. "A Look into the Heart of Darkness: A View of *Deliverance.*" In De La Fuente 59-64.

Taylor, Welford D. "Dickey Pursues Universal Truths in *Alnilam.*" *The Richmond News Leader.* 2 September 1987. 15.

Towers, Robert. "Prometheus Blind." *New York Times Book Review.* 21 June 1987. 7.

Tucker, Charles C. "Knowledge Up, Down, and Beyond: Dickey's 'The Driver' and 'Falling'." *CEA Critic* 38, no.4 (1976): 4-10.

Van Ness, A. Gordon. "Steering to the Morning Land: The Poet as Redeemer in Dickey's *The Zodiac*." *James Dickey Newsletter* 2 (Fall 1985): 2-10.

Van Ness, Gordon. "'Stand Waiting, My Love, Where You Are': Women in James Dickey's Early Poetry." *James Dickey Newsletter* 6 (Fall 1989): 2-11.

—. "'Up from the Human Down-beat': Double-Vision and Elemental Complicity in James Dickey's *The Eagle's Mile*." In Kirschten, ed.

—. "*Wayfarer: A Voice from the Southern Mountains*." *James Dickey Newsletter* 5 (Spring 1989): 31-33.

—. "'When Memory Stands without Sleep': James Dickey's War Years." *James Dickey Newsletter* 4 (Fall 1987): 2-13.

Varn, Jim. "Primordial Reunions: Motion in James Dickey's Early Poetry." *James Dickey Newsletter* 5 (Fall 1988): 4-14.

Waggoner, Hyatt H. *American Poets: From the Puritans to the Present*. Boston: Houghton Mifflin, 1968.

Wagner, Linda. "*Deliverance*: Initiation and Possibility." *South Carolina Review* 10 (April 1978): 49-55.

Warren, Robert Penn. "A Poem about the Ambition of Poetry: *The Zodiac*." *New York Times Book Review*. 14 November 1976. 8.

Weatherby, H.L. "The Way of Exchange in James Dickey's Poetry." *Sewanee Review* 74 (Summer 1966): 669-80.

Weigl, Bruce, and T.R. Hummer, eds. *The Imagination as Glory: The Poetry of James Dickey*. Urbana and Chicago: U of Illinois Press, 1984.

Whalin, Kathleen D. "*Bronwen, the Traw, and the Shape-Shifter*." *School Library Journal* 33 (October 1986): 173.

Wimsatt, Margaret. "*Self-Interviews*." *Commonweal* 93 (19 February 1971): 501-3.

Winchell, Mark Royden. "The River Within: Primitivism in James Dickey's *Deliverance*." *West Virginia University Philological Papers* 23 (January 1977): 106-14.

Yardley, Jonathan. "A Colossal Ornament?: *Jericho: The South Beheld*." *New Republic* (30 November 1974): 43-44.

Zweig, Paul. "Bel Canto, American Style: *The Strength of Fields*." *New York Times Book Review*. 6 January 1980. 6, 17.

Index